PARK CITY BAPTIST CHURCH
PARK CITY, KENTUCKY

Living at Peace
in a Turbulent World

Living at Peace in a Turbulent World

Henry Allen Parker

BROADMAN PRESS
Nashville, Tennessee

Library of Congress Catalog Card Number: 72–97603
Dewey Decimal Classification: 248.4
Printed in the United States of America

Preface

This book was born in my regular pulpit and radio ministry. The messages contained herein have either been delivered over a local radio station or from the pulpit of Orlando's First Baptist Church. As a pastor, my heart has been exceedingly burdened over the chaotic conditions in our world. It is my firm conviction that the Word of God and a genuine Christian testimony both are most relevant to man's needs in today's world. In these messages I have tried to be "relevant" and to speak to the great issues with which we are all confronted.

Our church carries on a continuous radio and television ministry. In addition, for over twelve years, I have had the privilege of participating in a radio program sponsored by a local bank. This program consists of brief, pointed messages relating to human need in our day. The gracious response of the listening audience, visible and invisible, has been a great factor in the decision to publish this book.

To say that this is "my book" would be incorrect. Too many different people have made a contribution to my personal life and to the content of these messages for me to claim absolute originality. Across the years I have gathered ideas, illustrations, etc. from many sources. Some of these have been long since forgotten. Many different writers, ministers, and church members have helped in so many ways that it would be impossible to list them all. But to them all I express my sincere gratitude. My sincere hope and prayer as this book goes forth is that God will use it to help many people "live at peace" in a very turbulent but exciting age.

Contents

I.

The Greatest Event of History

(John 3:16)

Several years ago Fulton Oursler wrote a best seller on the life of Christ entitled, *The Greatest Story Ever Told*. Literally millions of people have read and loved this book. It has appeared in book form, in series form in numerous newspapers, and even in serial form on major radio networks. The book becomes far more meaningful when one knows the circumstances under which it was written.

The story is told that Fulton Oursler was an agnostic in his early days, not believing in the existence of God, the veracity of the Bible, Jesus Christ, or his church. Mr. Oursler was a highly trained and talented writer. He used his pen in attacking religion as if it had been dipped in acid. In his attacks, he seemed to be utterly sincere and determined to do his best to destroy the fundamentals of Christianity. As a part of this effort, he decided to write a novel presenting his beliefs. In order to be as thorough as possible, he began to read the Bible and even made a trip to the Holy Land where he could see the sacred shrines and places where Jesus was supposed to have walked. He spent many months in the Holy Land doing spade work. Returning to America, he sat down and began to write. His first few chapters comprised a bitter attack on God, Christ, and religion. But in the process of writing, he became convicted by God's Spirit and then was converted to Christianity. After his conversion he destroyed what he had already written and began anew to write the book, *The Greatest Story Ever Told*. And the gist of this marvelous story is given in capsule form in 25 wonderful words:

For God so loved the world, that he gave his only begotten
Son, that whosoever believeth in him should not perish,
but have everlasting life (John 3:16).

Without any question this is the greatest single verse about the
greatest single event recorded in the Word of God. It has received
manifold treatment. R. G. Lee analyzed the passage this way:

Some have spoken of this verse as showing the celestial
origin of God's love, the sinful objects of God's love, the
sacrificial outlet of God's love, the simple offer of God's
love.

Some have written and spoken of this text as a verse
of seven clusters, namely:

The Great God, spoken of in the word, "God";

The Great Love, shown in the words, "so loved";

The Great Company, testified to in the words, "The
world";

The Great Gift, mightily evidenced in the words, "That
he gave his only begotten Son";

The Great Invitation, extended in the words, "That
whosoever believeth in him";

The Great Promise, given in the words, "Should not
perish";

The Great Possession, guaranteed to sinful humanity
in the words, "everlasting life."

Some have spoken of this verse as showing the circle
of God's love—its upward source, its downward sweep,
its outward sign, its onward security.[1]

John 3:16 is perhaps the first verse that most people learn when
they start memorizing Scripture verses. John, the beloved disciple,
records the words, but they were actually spoken by Jesus himself.
There are many things that John wrote in his Gospel, but none

compare with the brilliance of this one. There are some Scripture verses that are beautiful to repeat, easy to learn, hard to forget, and beyond human understanding. This is one of them! The truths contained speak for themselves. When we face it, we feel like removing our shoes from off our feet because we know that the ground whereon we stand is holy ground. No man really is adequate to comprehend fully its contents. Let us simply look at them.

I. THE ASSERTION—"GOD SO LOVED"

This first tells us what we need to know about God! Is it not marvelous that Jesus taught us many things about the Father and the greatest of these is the fact presented in this verse? To say that "God so loved the world" presents a truth that needs to be analyzed and then claimed by all the world.

GOD LOVES! There is no greater proclamation than this in any piece of literature. It is said that Martin Luther, the father of the Reformation, called this verse "The Little Gospel!" He loved it so much that when he lay on his deathbed, he repeated the verse distinctly three times in Latin. There is no more attractive theme to the average person than that of "love."

> The world is dying for a little bit of love
> Everywhere we hear the sighing for a little bit of love
> Love that rights a wrong, fills the heart with hope and
>   song,
> They have waited, oh, so long, for a little bit of love

There are no more thrilling or important words that can be spoken by a loved one than these three, "I love you." All people feel that it is marvelous to be loved by anyone in our family and other human relationships.

Dr. A. C. Archibald, in *Man to Man,* tells the following story. Captain Connely of the Near East Relief, told about a little Near

Eastern waif, one of thousands who slept on the floor of the great barracks. The Captain came along one night on a tour of inspection to see if the children were all right. This little girl was crying softly to herself. Both her parents were dead; she had no relatives. Connely stooped over and said: "Are you sick, dear?" "No, Sir," said the child. "Have you had enough to eat?" "Oh, yes, Sir." "Then what is the matter, child?" "Oh, Sir, Sir! I want someone to love me. I am all alone."

Yes, it is good to be loved by people. The most thrilling thing that can be said about love, however, is the fact that God loves. There is no theme in the Bible emphasized more than this. One of the most beautiful expressions is found in Romans 5:6–8:

> For when we were yet without strength, in due time Christ died for the ungodly. For scarcely for a righteous man will one die: Yet peradventure for a good man some would even dare to die. But God commendeth his love toward us, in that, while we were yet sinners, Christ died for us.

Indeed, we do "stand amazed in the presence of Jesus the Nazarene, and wonder how he could love me, a sinner, condemned, unclean." The Eternal God, the Father and Ruler *loves*—so proclaims the Word of God.

GOD LOVES ALL! The Scripture states "the world." This means all who are in the world—the good and the bad, the rich and the poor, the young and old, the saved and the lost. His love is all inclusive; none are omitted. Dr. Theodore F. Adams, pastor emeritus, First Baptist Church, Richmond, Virginia, tells the story of how, many years ago in a midwestern orphanage, there was a little girl whose body was deformed and whose face was far from beautiful. Visitors wanted to adopt the handsome little boys and golden haired little girls, but no one wanted this unfortunate and unattractive little child. One day a fine mother, whose child had died and whose life now seemed empty, told the superintendent of her desire to adopt a child that no one else wanted. The superintendent informed her that there was one little girl whose prayers for a home of her own had been unanswered. Can you imagine the scene that followed as the heartbroken mother held out her arms toward the little girl nobody wanted and said: "I have come for you!"

Dr. Adams relates how that years later the inspector of the orphanages of that particular state in a routine report wrote: "I had a wonderful evening in one of the cottages of the orphanage. The matron there is especially beloved by her children. I was there just after the supper hour, and the children gathered around her chair, and they all sang and talked together. Some of them stroked her hair and others just sat close by. She is deformed physically, but in her eyes there was a radiance and a light that transformed the life of that cottage and those boys and girls." The little girl nobody wanted had grown up and now made her life mean to others what someone who loved her had once meant to her. This is like the love which Jesus Christ has for the world of people. He loves us in spite of our unattractiveness, our failures, our rebellious spirits, and our indifference to him. *God loves each!* It is not enough to say that God loves and that he loves all, but we must realize that he loves each person individually. The "whosoever" is a universal term, but it also singles out the individual. Here the individual is not lost in the multitude, and in order to clarify and give us this assurance, Jesus said "whosoever." Richard Baxter, commenting upon this verse of Scripture, once said, "Thank God for that 'whosoever'! There are many Richard Baxters in the world, and if he had singled out a Richard Baxter, I would not have known for sure that he was talking about me. This way when he used the word, 'whosoever,' I know that term includes me."

II. THE EXPRESSION OF GOD'S LOVE—"HE GAVE"

Love will express itself. It becomes the motivating power which propels one into action. The fruits of love are easily seen. Since God genuinely loves man, then he must do something about it. The Bible tells us in Genesis 6:5–6: "And God saw that the wickedness of man was great in the earth, and that every imagination of the thoughts of his heart was only evil continually, and it repented the Lord that he had made man on the earth, and it grieved him at his heart." Grief is a love word. Grief and love go together; you cannot separate the two. Since God possessed a strong love for man, then he was grieved because of man's sin. That same love projected down across the centuries ultimately resulted in the sacrifice of "the only begotten Son of God."

This same principle applies in human relationships. When husband and wife really love each other, they will endeavor in every way possible to express that love. There is no such thing as true love without a genuine desire to express that love through sacrifice and giving. There is something wrong with a love that is selfish and inconsiderate.

The love of God as expressed through the death of Christ is the most Perfect Gift ever made to man. On the human plane we present material gifts to each other with the full realization that they do not last. The gifts that last are the spiritual ones. The thing that God did for man on Calvary cannot be compared with a material thing since the issues are spiritual and are eternal.

There are two ways to determine the inherent value of a gift. First, its evaluation by the giver. Try to look at God's gift through the eyes of God. The Bible speaks of Christ as "the only begotten Son of God." The heart of any parent instantly responds to such a statement. Surely this is the ultimate, supreme gift. One reads the story of Abraham's obedience to God in offering his son, Isaac, with deep concern because of the sacrifice involved. How infinitely more meaningful is the gift of God's Son for a lost world! How much did it really cost God to give his Son? Is there anywhere in all of the Bible a record of God's ever having sacrificed or given anything that meant much to him prior to this experience? Why did he do it? There is only one answer to that and it must arise out of his measureless love for man. Surely the poet is right when he sings:

> Were the whole realm of nature mine,
>   That were a present far too small;
> Love so amazing, so divine,
>   Demands my love, my life, my all.

Second, evaluation is determined by what a gift means to the receiver. Ask yourself the question: What does the sacrifice of Jesus Christ really mean to me? The Lord says in John 10:10–11: "The thief cometh not, but for to steal, and to kill, and to destroy: I am come that they might have life, and that they might have it more abundantly. I am the good shepherd: the good shepherd giveth his life for the sheep." Paul says in 2 Corinthians 8:9: "For ye know the grace of our Lord Jesus Christ, that, though he was rich, yet for your sakes he became poor, that ye through his poverty might be rich." By far the grandest and most meaningful gift ever made to and for any man is that which God presents through Jesus Christ.

III. THE RECEPTION OF GOD'S GIFT—"WHOSOEVER BELIEVETH"

Remember the design, the assertion concerning God's love—it is intended for anyone and everyone who will receive it. "For God so loved the world that he gave his only begotten Son that *whosoever* believeth in him should not perish." In Revelation 22:17, God says: "And the spirit and the bride say, Come. And let him that heareth say, Come. And let him that is athirst come. And whosoever will, let him take the water of life freely." The invitation of the Master is: "Come unto me all ye that labor and are heavy laden and I will give you rest. Take my yoke upon you, and learn of me;

for I am meek and lowly in heart: and ye shall find rest unto your souls."

Although the gift is designed for everyone, still it is a gift that must be received. It can only be received through personal faith in Jesus Christ. Since sinful man cannot save himself, God has come down in Jesus Christ to save him. Man might not be able to save himself, but he can believe in Jesus Christ. Believe is something that everyone can do, if he so desires. Indeed, salvation can come in no other way. Ebenezer Wooten, eccentric Scottish preacher, closed a revival meeting on a village green many years ago. As he was removing his tent, a young man came rushing up to inquire, "Mr. Wooten, what must I do to be saved?" The evangelist replied: "Absolutely nothing, young man! You are too late." The troubled young man then said: "What do you mean I'm too late? Isn't there any chance of my being saved?" The great preacher replied: "I did not say that, son. You asked me what *you* must do. My answer was that 'there is nothing you can do.' Jesus did it all when he died on Calvary. All you must do is simply accept what he did for you long ago."

Man must receive Jesus Christ in order to have eternal life. Jesus said to Nicodemus: "Ye must be born again." In this greatest event of history, God provided salvation for man because of man's need. The hymn writer has beautifully expressed it in these words:

"I heard the voice of Jesus say, 'Come unto me and rest;
Lay down, thou weary one, lay down thy head upon my
    breast.'
I came to Jesus as I was, weary, and worn, and sad;
I found in him a resting-place, and he has made me glad."

IV. THE GOAL OF GOD'S GIFT—"ETERNAL LIFE"

John 3:16 tells us much about the future—"should not perish, but have everlasting life."

The "unbeliever" is perishing. The word "perishing" is often used in connection with extreme hunger or thirst. The Bible proclaims that Jesus is both "bread and water." People without him are starving and thirsting to death. One does not have to wait until physical death in order to perish. The Scriptures say: "He that believeth not is condemned already."

The "believer" is inheriting "eternal life." This is a quality of life which only God can impart. It is not a gift of a temporary nature, but is eternal. This means that it is a priceless possession. It is not life for a moment, a day, a year, but—*eternal* life. "He that heareth my words and believeth on him that sent me hath everlasting life and shall not come into condemnation, but is passed from death unto life." The quality of this life is beautifully expressed by the Master in his words to Martha:

> "Jesus saith unto her, 'Thy brother shall rise again.' Martha saith unto him, 'I know that he shall rise again in the resurrection at the last day.' Jesus said unto her, 'I am the resurrection and the life: he that believeth in me, though he were dead, yet shall he live: And whosoever liveth and believeth in me shall never die. Believest thou this?' " (John 11:23–26).

Surely this is a desirable gift which each person must appropriate for himself. There is a beautiful story in connection with John 3:16, concerning an experience of the great preacher, Dwight L. Moody, when he was a chaplain during the Civil War. It seems that he visited a dying soldier in a hospital camp back of the lines at the Battle of Gettysburg. As he ministered to the wounded boys, he came upon this particular, fine-looking lad lying desperately wounded. Because of his condition and also his wonderful personality, Mr. Moody was attracted to him and did his best to comfort him. Moody asked him whether or not he knew the Lord. The soldier boy regretfully informed him that he did not, but that he had a good Christian mother, and loved her very much. Moody tried to lead the young man to Christ, but soon decided that it was best not to talk further with him since he seemed to be so weak. Before leaving, he read him the story of the interview of Jesus with Nicodemus recorded in the third chapter of John. When he came to the sixteenth verse: "For God so loved the world, . . ." the boy's eyes suddenly opened wide. He inquired: "Is that in the Bible?" Assured that it was, the boy then pleaded, "Would you mind reading it again?" Mr. Moody did so very slowly this time. The boy requested that Moody read it again for the third time. As he did so, the boy's eyes closed and knowing the end was close at hand, Moody prayed a brief prayer and then went his way. He requested the nurse call him if the boy revived. When Moody came back on his regular rounds, he wanted especially to check on the young man. When he came to the cot, it was vacant, but splotched with blood. The nurse said to him, with tears in her eyes: "Chaplain, I wish you had been here a little while ago. Just before that young man to whom you were talking last night passed on, I noticed his lips moving as if he were trying to say something. I put my ear down to his lips to hear what he was saying, and found that he was repeating over and over the words, 'God so loved the world, that he gave his only begotten Son, that whosoever believeth in him, should not perish, but have everlasting life.' I saw the end was near, and asked if he wished to leave any message, and he just whispered, 'Tell my mother I died trusting Jesus Christ as my Saviour,' and then he was gone." What a joy that message must have brought to the mother's heart. It was made possible because of the greatest story concerning the greatest gift and event in history!

With Jesus Christ as the foundation of life, then one is prepared not only for death but to make life here and now most meaningful.

BUILDINGS TO MATCH FOUNDATIONS

An old-timer stood on the street corner one day talking with a close friend. Pointing to a building across the street, he said to his friend, "That building standing there is only two stories high, as you can see. Well, it is a lot like people I know. It is a two-story building on a ten-story foundation. When it was being built, the owner had the idea that he would build a ten-story building, and ordered the foundation put in with that in mind. Then something happened and he never built more than two stories." That old gentleman was absolutely right! There are a lot of two-story men all about us who have ten-story foundations. The greatest tragedies of life are the people who are living below their possibilities.

When God said, "Let us make man in our image," this gave to man the crowning compliment of all of God's creation. No other creature on earth can approach him. He can think, dream, aspire, hope, build, and make progress. Endowed with talents unequaled, he walks through life, the towering triumph of all that lives. It is tragic but true that humanity has never yet realized what his capacities actually are. Occasionally some person, referred to as a genius, rises above the average. The astonishing thing is that many psychologists maintain that the capacity for genius is within each man and woman if he can but call it forth.

The writer of the book of Proverbs solemnly asserts that the man who wastes is as much a sinner as the one who destroys. In other words, the one who wastes life is as guilty as the one who takes it.

Our world is cursed with smallness—small talk, small interest, small ambitions, small plans, small faith, and small living. Even though our world geographically has shrunk to a small neighborhood, many of us find it impossible to become interested in anything that happens outside of our immediate community. The entertainment world, with the whole range of human emotions and experiences to draw upon, contents itself with the dreary monotony of sex and filth. Our world presents so much by way of beauty and challenge, and yet multitudes of people are content to live in the gutter and never feel or attempt anything big.

"Build thee more stately mansions, O my soul."

---

[1] R. G. Lee, *A Greater Than Solomon* (Nashville: Broadman Press, 1935), p. 115.

2.

"Take a Look at Yourself"

(Isaiah 6:1–8)

Among the multitudinous problems bugging most people today, and especially our young folk, is the problem of identity. The search for identity! What is the meaning of life? Who am I? Why am I here? Where did I come from? Where am I going?

When you study the problem, you will be amazed to discover that it is not a new one. It's always been a problem—the search for identity.

Paul said in 2 Corinthians 13:5, "Examine yourselves, whether ye be in the faith; prove your own selves. Know ye not your own selves, how that Jesus Christ is in you, except ye be reprobates [or unless you fail to meet the test]?"

This is precisely what Isaiah did as he stood in the temple and had a vision of God. He looked at his own life as well as at those around him. Long ago, Socrates said, "The unexamined life is not worth living." I am confident that he was talking about convictions, motives for living, and sacrifices, and he spoke words of wisdom far beyond even his day.

You and I live in a day when we understand what it means to undergo tests or examinations. Tests are made everywhere—on the soil, on fabrics, the food that we eat, water that we drink, machines that we operate, air that we breathe.

Human beings undergo tests. Periodically we have a "checkup" and organs are examined, physical stamina is determined, emotional reactions and one's intellectual ability—all of these are tested, examined very carefully by well-trained physicians.

But, a most needed examination often is ignored—*self-examina-*

tion. The Bible presses the necessity of:

Self knowledge: "When Simon Peter saw it, he fell down at Jesus' knees, saying, Depart from me; for I am a sinful man, O Lord" *(Luke 5:8).*

Self reverence: "What! know ye not that your body is the temple of the Holy Ghost which is in you, which ye have of God, and ye are not your own?" *(1 Cor. 6:19).*

Self control: "But I keep under my body, and bring it into subjection; lest that by any means, when I have preached to others, I myself should be a castaway" *(1 Cor. 9:27).*

It was Tennyson who said, "Self-knowledge, self-reverence and self-control: these three alone lead life to sovereign power."

But, this three-fold cord will snap if you do not weave into it another strand that is stronger and more meaningful. In Romans 6 Paul admonishes:

> Likewise reckon ye also yourselves to be dead indeed unto sin, but alive unto God through Jesus Christ our Lord.
>
> Let not sin therefore reign in your mortal body, that ye should obey it in the lusts thereof.
>
> Neither yield ye your members as instruments of unrighteousness unto sin: but yield yourselves unto God, as those that are alive from the dead, and your members as instruments of righteousness unto God.

This self-knowledge, self-reverence, self-control *must be Christ-controlled.* If life is to be harmonious, there is a three-fold relationship which must be taken into account. Our relationship to the world *about us,* our relationship to the world *above and beyond us,* and our relationship to the world that is *within us.*

I. SELF-KNOWLEDGE: "I AM A SINFUL MAN!"

One of the greatest tendencies of life is the inclination to pretense. Dr. Lofton Hudson has written a book entitled *Grace Is Not a Blue-Eyed Blonde*. In it he says that the usual definition of the word "hypocrite" is merely pretending to be something that a person is not. But even in that concept, that context, most of us are deceitful, he points out. Everyone of us, for instance, has a mask—a front or a facade which he shows to others. At the same time he has a real self which only he and his God know. As we become aware that we are relaters in a relationship with others, we become self-conscious, and then begin to prepare a face, and then the outward mask. The mask is symbolically presented in the Genesis story of God's clothing of Adam and Eve in the Garden of Eden. There is a self that we present to the world while at the same time there is a split, a division, a plurality, a self which only we know and God knows.

Sometimes, psychotherapy, as Dr. Hudson says, may help us individually to peer behind this screen and see what truly motivates us—in spite of what we put up or what we claim and to really know ourselves.[1]

Bobby Burns, the great poet, sat in church one day. Right in front of him, according to the story, was a precise little woman. Just the way she held her head and the way her hat was perched on her hair, and the way she would gingerly touch her hair to see that everything was in place, attracted his attention. As he watched, he saw a louse crawl out from under her hat and down the back of her neck, and supposedly this became the inspiration for his now famous poem, "To a Louse."

Look at yourself! Socrates was the one who said: "Know thyself!" Years later, somebody added to that, "The proper study of mankind is man." Then we should begin with ourselves.

Failure to do this is a lack of effort on our part, or a desire to blame others with our failures, our shortcomings. The secret of making a success of life usually lies in the individual, not in the power nor in the hands of anyone else. No wonder the poet has said:

> Not in the clamour of the crowded street
> > Nor in the shouts and plaudits of the throng
> But in ourselves, are the triumphs and defeats.

In Julius Caesar, Cassius has come to the sobering realization that he and his contemporaries have not made the most of their opportunities. Here is his forthright confession: "The fault, dear Brutus, is not in our stars, BUT IN OURSELVES, that we are underlings."

This is indeed a disarming declaration! Our generation has become proficient in the art of self-justification. When things go wrong, when they are not as we desire them to be, we love to accuse circumstances and other people and blame them with our failures.

Florence Nightingale, the patron saint of nurses, overcame many frustrating circumstances and incredible obstacles in order to carry out her life's vocation, and near the end of the way made a tremendous statement when she said: "Life is never decided so much by circumstance, as by inner-stance."

One understands himself when he knows all his capacities and limitations. Without ignoring them, without glossing over them, we need to face and understand them. Really, we are the only ones who can know. Other people might analyze and try to help us along the way, but we are the only ones who can know.

A fellow in an asylum was visited by the psychiatrist, who noticed that one fellow was sitting over on the side of the room alone, scratching himself. He kept it up for a long time until the psychiatrist finally decided to go over and engage him in conversation. He said to him: "Sir, I wonder if you would mind telling me why you just sit here scratching yourself all the time?"

"Because," he said, "I am the only one in the world who knows where I itch!"

He had something there. Our trouble is, most of us do not really face ourselves and try to understand as God intended us to understand ourselves, so as to reach the highest pinnacle of our possibilities. And we don't want anybody trying to tell us about ourselves.

A friend went to visit a man who had been ill for a long time. The old man was back in the kitchen brewing a pot of coffee, so he went in and sat down with him. As they began talking the friend looked up at a shelf and noticed a long line of medicine bottles, all of them the kind of medicines anyone can walk into a drugstore and buy. He finally said to the man, "Well, haven't you gotten any good out of any of this medicine?" The old man said, "No, I've tried them all and can't find anything to do me any good."

So the fellow said: "Well, why don't you forget about all these bottles and go to a doctor somewhere who can tell you what's wrong with you and get you on the road to recovery?"

"Oh, I'm not going to any of those fellows! He'd tell me what's really wrong with me, and I don't want to know!" [2]

And the tragedy about life is that too many of us feel exactly the same way. We are not willing to know our capabilities and our limitations.

Know yourself *mentally.* Know thyself, is the admonition, from an intellectual point of view. Shakespeare, in Hamlet, said:

> What a piece of work is a man; how noble in reason,
> how infinite in faculty, in form and movement, how ex-
> press and admirable; in apprehension how like an angel;
> in action, how like a god; the beauty of the world, the
> paragon of animals.

He was talking about man's intellectual capacities. You and I know that the battle of life is waged not by brute strength, but by one's intellectual capacities, with the help and the grace of Almighty God. Everything that we have in life today, almost without exception, is a result of ideas—man's ability to reason or to think.

Know yourself *physically*. What a tragedy that so many of us do not care for our bodies. Willfully and deliberately we take things into the body that will destroy the mind and that will shorten the span of life. My friend, this is what Paul is talking about when he speaks of "staying on top of his body," controlling it, knowing his strength and his weaknesses. No general would go into battle without a knowledge of the army that is at his back, and so God's Word admonishes us to examine ourselves, and when we thus examine ourselves and understand ourselves, we discover then the key to redemption and the key to life. This might be a painful process. Indeed, it often is.

Think about the prodigal son. It was a rather painful process through which he passed, but the Bible tells us that he came to himself. Now, that can be the Great Divide in life, the prelude to fulfilment in Jesus Christ. A person must be willing to look at himself and really see himself, even as Peter saw himself in the presence of Christ, or as Isaiah saw himself in the presence of God in the temple.

II. SELF-REVERENCE: "YOUR BODY IS THE TEMPLE"

Along with self-knowledge must go self-reverence. Paul said: "Know ye not that your body is the temple of God. . . ." The importance of self-reverence is more clearly seen when you look at a person who has lost all sense of self-respect and see what happens to him as a result. When he loses his appreciation for his true nature and value, as a usual thing despair sets in, faith is gone, and hope is blighted.

Mark Rutherford said a rather significant thing one day: "Contempt from those about us is hard to bear, but God help the poor wretch who contemns himself."

The contempt of others is hard to bear, but God have mercy on the person who has a contempt for himself. You remember

Guinevere's sad wail: "O shut me round with narrowing nunnery-walls, Meek maidens from the voices crying, 'Shame!' I must not scorn myself." When I begin to scorn myself, that moment hope is dead.

Thank God that Jesus Christ, with his all-piercing wisdom and knowledge, knew what was in man; but in spite of that knowledge he never despaired and he never lost respect for a human being, and especially for the potentialities resident in that life.

So, how are you going to know the truth about yourself? In my opinion, as Dr. Maxwell Maltz points out, you are going to have to come, with psychology, to religion; and you're going to have to read what the Word of God has to say about the meaning and the purpose of life. After all, the Scriptures tell us that God created man a little lower than the angels.

Man was made in the image of God. When he breathed into his nostrils the breath of life, man became a living soul and God said to him, "Have dominion over the earth." And then we read the magnificent truth about Jesus Christ and how much he thought of human life, and how he said one day: "What doth it profit a man, if he gain the whole world, but lose his own soul." And then we see that Jesus placed such value upon life that he was willing to climb the cross and to die thereon.

Take a look at this creature which has come from the hands of the all-wise and all-powerful God.

Look at man and realize that the Creator would not turn out an inferior product anymore than a master painter would turn out an inferior canvas. Such a Creator would not deliberately engineer his product to fail, anymore than a manufacturer would deliberately build a failure into an automobile.

Dr. Leslie D. Weatherhead, the great English preacher, has said:

If we have in our minds the picture of ourselves as fear-haunted and defeated nobodies, we must get rid of that picture at once and hold up our heads. That is a false picture and the false must go. God sees us as men and women in whom and through whom he can do a great work. Surely he sees us as already serene, confident, and cheerful. He sees us not as pathetic victims of life, but masters of the art of living. Not wanting sympathy, but imparting help to others and therefore thinking less and less of ourselves and full, not of self-concern, but of love and laughter and the desire to serve our fellowman in the spirit of Christ.

Let us look at the real selves which we are in the making, the moment we believe in their existence. We must recognize the possibility of change, and believe in the self we are now in the process of becoming. That old sense of unworthiness and failure must go. It is false. We are not to believe in that which is false.

III. SELF-CONTROL: "I KEEP UNDER MY BODY"

Finally, it is tremendously important that we exercise self-control over our lives. Paul said, "I keep under my body." Plato depicted the human soul as a figure of a many-headed monster, a lion and a man, all combined in one being. The man represented the higher nature of man, his personality, his reason. The lion (the passionate element of man) and the many-headed monster (the lust and the appetites of his body). The point of it all is: Only when man rules is it well with the human soul. That is not unscriptural.

This is what the Bible says: "He that *ruleth his spirit* is better than he that taketh a city." Emerson wrote many popular short essays. One of them was entitled, "Self-reliance." All the way through that little essay, there are thoughts like these that ring over and over: "Trust thyself"; "Insist on yourself"; "Nothing can bring you peace but yourself." And it was Paul who said: "Let not sin therefore reign in your mortal body. . . ." Tennyson wrote many wonderful things, and he must have been a very deep believer. Speaking of King Arthur, he wrote:

> There grew great tracts of wilderness,
> Wherein the beast was ever more and more,
> But man was less and less, till Arthur came.
> . . . Then he drove
>   The heathen; after, slew the beast, and felled
>   The forest, letting in the sun, and made
>   Broad pathways for the hunter and the knight
>   And so returned.

"Wherein the beast was ever more and more, and man was less and less . . ." until Arthur came! What a picture of our own lives! *When Jesus Christ comes,* and when you crown him King in your life, he'll slay the beast, he'll drive out the foes that have conquered, he'll restore all of the waste places of the soul, and out of the wild confusions of the life bring forth settled peace and ordered beauty.

Now, read again Romans 6: "Neither YIELD ye your members as instruments of unrighteousness unto sin: but YIELD yourselves unto God. . . ."

The only way to control your life and all of its powers and potentialities and possibilities—the only way to control it—is to surrender it to the One who made it and who knows infinitely more about it than you will ever know; the One who is able to make it over into his liking and then to empower and to use it for his glory and for your own happiness. I appeal to you to surrender yourself to him—in self-knowledge, self-reverence, and in self-control.

Habit is a dynamic force in human life and plays a most important part in the building of character and in the forging of destiny.

BINDING CHAINS

On Highway 441, north of Ocala, Florida, there is a shopping center and animal display. For many months the proprietor kept a chained elephant under a little shed right out in front of the building. The striking thing about the elephant was the fact that he was at perfect liberty to go anywhere he pleased—within a radius of about fifteen feet. The elephant, being a wise animal, probably soon learned the hopelessness of tugging against his chain. Therefore, he wandered no more than fourteen feet, eleven inches from the stake to which he was tied. His keeper would assure people that the old fellow had become so accustomed to his chain that, even though it might be loosed and he might be actually free, still he would not venture more than fourteen feet from the central point.

All of us have seen other types of chained elephants—men of tremendous possibilities who were linked to slavery through some wasteful habit or debilitating weakness. Some of these men even will declare that they are perfectly free, but more than likely this is because they have never really tried to break their chains. They continue enjoying the freedom of fifteen feet; they refuse to be religious because they want to be free; and still they go on tramping around and around an appetite, a habit, a prejudice, or a weakness of some kind.

Habits become either chains or wings. The habit of frugality provides for comfort and security in old age, whereas the habit of spending usually leads to want and waste. The habit of using time frugally means the accomplishment of high purpose, but the habit of squandering time leads to poverty and failure, and yet, the psychological principles that underlie both kinds of habits are always the same. First comes the choice of action, then frequent repetition, and then the binding chain of regularity. The only time to change a habit is in the early stages. No man ever knows how free he is until he attempts to break a bad habit, to wrench himself loose from some old prejudice, or to tear up by the roots some old grudge. The presence and power of chains is readily discovered.

Wise and happy is the man who sets out to make his habits into wings that will enable him to rise above the binding power of chains.

DREDGING

"Wash me thoroughly from my iniquity, and cleanse me from my sin" (Ps. 51:2).

Somewhere I read the story that the city of Shanghai is located nearly twenty miles back from the sea, on the river Whangpoo. It is a sluggish stream of water that slips down from the plains of the interior, and bears a vast quantity of mud and silt. The great ocean liners that dock at Shanghai make their way up the river in order to discharge their freight and passengers in the heart of the great city.

A familiar sight along the riverbank is that of a dredge sucking up the debris from the riverbed and dumping it onto a barge to be carried out to sea. The natives will tell you that the old river brings so much mud from the plains that the river channel would be filled in no time if they did not keep it dredged out.

Herein lies a remarkable parable: So many streams flow into the human mind, bringing in mud, filth, trifles, and pettiness, that a person has to keep dredging continually in order to keep the channels of his mind deep enough to allow great ideas to anchor there.

News media can easily divert a stream of mud into the mind —divorces, scandal, gossip, crime, tumult, riots, mob action, vulgarity, etc. As fine as it is to have a newspaper, the person who depends upon it for his education is superficial indeed. If he has no other source for inspiration and ideas, then he lives in a very poor world.

Entertainment media of the day also divert such a stream of mud into the mind that a person must be on guard. Sensuality, sex perversion, indecency, paganism—what a pollution these become to the unwary soul exposed to them continually.

Such streams as these have the effect of filling up the mind and heart in such a way that the beautiful, the true, the lovely, the holy, and the great find it impossible to get anchorage. No man can hope to live a happy and constructive life who does not keep his mind dredged to make room for the reception of the wholesome and good.

---

[1] R. Lofton Hudson, *Grace Is Not a Blue-Eyed Blonde* (Waco, Texas: Word Books, 1968), p. 38.

[2] Lee MacBride White, *How to Know Yourself,* p. 46.

3.

Guidebook for Living

(2 Timothy 3)

Herman Gockel tells us about a unique experience of two high school girls on a hot summer afternoon. The day was Sunday, and the girls leisurely strolled along through the downtown section of their city. Suddenly they found themselves directly in front of a huge old church building. Looking at the lofty stained-glass window which their art teacher had told them to be sure to see, one of them stopped short and grunted: "Nothing beautiful in that! Just a lot of dirty glass." It happened that there was a little old lady who overheard the remark. She walked up to the girls and said: "You can't judge the beauty of an art glass window from the outside. Why don't you step inside?" They did, and before they knew it, they were standing motionless and enthralled, their faces bathed in a symphony of color which was pouring from the stained-glass window. The little lady was right: "You just can't judge a stained-glass window from the outside."

Let us take an object lesson. What about the Bible? If you really want to know if the Bible is God's Word, there is only one way to find out: "Go inside." There are many fine arguments, logical proofs, compelling evidence based on historical study; but these will not mean nearly as much as a reverent reading of the Book itself. Actually, the strongest evidence that the Bible has been given to us by God is one which cannot be passed from one man to another. It is a *conviction* which the Holy Spirit pours into the hearts of those who "go inside"—of those who read the Book and place themselves under its converting and empowering influence. To be sure, there are other evidences of the Bible's divine authorship.

In more than 2,000 instances, the Bible identifies itself as the Word of God. Again and again its prophecies have been fulfilled. The Son of God placed his stamp of divine approval on the Scriptures. Throughout the whole wide world wherever the Bible has gone, it has left a trail of blessing. All of these are valid ways of "proving" that the Bible is God's Word; but, like our high school girls to whom we referred, it is possible to discuss all these proofs while standing on the outside of the Book and thus to miss the greatest proof of all—the witness of the Holy Spirit through the power of the Word itself. The best advice to the honest inquirer about the Bible is to go inside. That is where its beauty can be seen.

Some time ago, in one of the departments of our Sunday School, there was a survey, inviting the people to express their thinking—about what the church is doing or not doing, which they like or dislike, and what they can do in order to make a greater contribution to the work of our Lord through the church.

The one key word in the evaluation was *relevance*—relevance of the church to the twentieth century, relevance of the Word of God. Let us face frankly the fact that there is a mounting chorus of critics saying the church is irrelevant. There are people today who have concluded that all of our activity is "full of sound and fury, signifying nothing." For these people, the church already has lost her relevancy, and to a great degree ceased to be effective in the pressing needs of the twentieth century. Or, to express it as one did recently: "The church today is an island of irrelevant piety surrounded by an ocean of secular need!"

The critics are many, and their criticisms are very sharp. They are very severe. But, thank God, on the horizon today there is a general spirit of effort at renewal, redirection, and revival. What is the relevancy of the Word of God, the Bible, in our day and in our generation? What do we say about the Bible?

The New Hampshire Confession of Faith, drawn up in 1852, states the position to which Baptists have more or less adhered to for over a hundred years:

> We believe the Holy Bible was written by men divinely
> inspired, and is a perfect treasury of heavenly instruction.
> That it has God for its author, salvation for its end, and
> truth without any mixture of error for its matter; that it
> reveals the principles by which God will judge us, and
> therefore is and shall remain to the end of the world, the
> true center of Christian union and the supreme standard
> by which all human conduct, creeds and opinions should
> be tried.

Dr. W. R. White, one of the greats of Southern Baptist life, and
for many years president of Baylor University, put it this way:

> The Christian faith and life must have an authoritative
> criterion or tested standard of measure. In order to be of
> value it must be reliable. It cannot be left to the whim,
> the fancies, the prejudices of men. We do have unchanging
> criterion—THE DIVINE REVELATION OF GOD—
> the record of which is THE BIBLE.

That is what we say we believe. But, let's see now, do we really?
Do we really?

I. OUR PREDICAMENT

Actually, the problems of contemporary society grow largely out
of the fact of our disobedience to the Word of God in so many
particulars. Never, in all the history of the world, has mankind
been more adept at self-analysis, or better equipped to deal with
his own predicament than at the present time. In this nuclear age
man is painfully, agonizingly aware that there is something tragically wrong with him, and with his world. Skilled analysts are able

to describe to us man's condition, but they are utterly helpless to give us a clear formula and guide to lead us out of "the mess" that we are in.

Our world rushes pell-mell into the gathering shades of unhappiness, turmoil and darkness, neglecting its most important source of truth and life—the revealed Word of God. And yet, the Bible *screams* at us, jumps down off the shelf and dusts itself off, and cries for attention, because man, unaided it teaches us, can no more understand, accept, or cure his malady or his illness than an insane person can deal with his own derangement, or a man with a ruptured appendix can effectively operate on himself. God, through biblical revelation, makes known man's nature, what he is, and what he can become through the power of God.

But though we say the Bible is authoritative, we just don't practice its precepts.

Here is an important incident that occurred 2,000 years ago, in the life of Jesus:

"And in the synagogue there was a man, which had a spirit of an unclean devil, and cried out with a loud voice, saying, Let us alone; what have we to do with thee, thou Jesus of Nazareth? art thou come to destroy us? I know thee who thou art; the Holy One of God" (Luke 4:33–34).

That is the question of a crazy man, but I assure you that it is not a crazy man's question, because it is the fundamental inquiry of all humanity in our day. The question is, "Does Jesus really matter?" "Is the Word of God really relevant to modern life?" We readily can understand how our forefathers, when life was so difficult and the wilderness was beset with all kinds of dangers, were so dependent on God. They instinctively turned to God. But why do we need him in our generation, with its multitudinous laws for our protection, with its highly specialized modes of education and its medical knowledge and skills, with its airborne cushions of comfort and ease? What on earth does a Galilean peasant who lived 2,000 years ago have to do with modern life? He doesn't even understand the problems under which we labor!

Too often we use the Bible for everything under heaven, except perhaps for the purpose for which it was given us. The following searching article came to my attention recently:

> From Genesis I we have learned that evolution is false, and we feel that we have successfully answered the evolutionists. We have led a crusade to defend the authority of Scripture against the attacks of science. We have written literally hundreds of books debating whether the days of creation lasted 24 hours, whether the species of biology correspond to the "kinds" of Genesis, etc.
>
> We have added to our statements of faith to make clear that man is a special creation; argued about the contents of the Bible and when Jesus is coming again, and how he is coming, to the point that in the estimate of many people in the world, it has become ridiculous.

When you think of "relevance," what do you think of? I have an idea that you think about Black Panthers, pollution, the Beatles, demonstrations, hunger, Marshall McLuhan, and Martin Luther King. Different people will think of different things, but there is one thing of which you can be sure, no one will think of—the Old Testament.

When we think of the Old Testament, we think of a book written thousands of years ago about people who had never heard of electricity or trains or printing presses, let alone atomic energy and rockets and television. What could such an old book tell us? In the midst of all the Old Testament's talk about shittim wood and cubits and wave offerings and begatting, there are some interesting stories (like David and Goliath), but they certainly aren't very significant or relevant.

However, evangelicals believe that the Bible is the final authority for faith and practice. We believe that the Bible has the answers for all human problems.

But what does that mean in relation to the Old Testament? Evangelicals see that stories about Moses and David are more than stories—more even than true stories. They teach us, for example, to trust in God no matter what the odds. Of course, the importance of the Old Testament is primarily spiritual.

We live in a different dispensation and the world has changed so much that we can't expect to learn much from the Old Testament about poverty or racism or justice.

Right?

Wrong! So wrong it is hard to believe we have ever read the Old Testament and even harder to believe that we accept it as our final authority. The truth is that chapter after chapter in the Old Testament is directly relevant to the contemporary situation. Surely Moses has more to say to today's issues than McLuhan and Marcuse combined. And Amos has more to say than Abbie Hoffman!

II. LISTEN TO THE BIBLE SPEAK ON CURRENT PROBLEMS

Paul, the great apostle, repeatedly said, "Preach the Word!" Do you know why? Because this Book is the most relevant word on earth to man and his life, and its significance is found in the fact that its truths are eternal and unchanging. They speak to the deepest levels of man's need. They are universal in their application, they declare the message of God's salvation. They confront mankind with the meaning and the demands of discipleship and they provoke a compassionate concern for the well-being of all men. They speak with authority and confidence to the issues of today.

Do they? Look at the first chapter of Genesis. What about the problem of *human relationships,* on the horizon of our world:

"And God said, Let us make man in our image, after our likeness: and let them have dominion over the fish of the sea and over the fowl of the air, and over the cattle, and over all the earth, and over every creeping thing that creepeth upon the earth. So God created man in his own image, in the image of God created he him; male and female created he them."

And if *one* is made in the image of God, that means *all* are made in the image of God. It teaches that all men have been made in God's image; therefore, red, yellow, black, and white—all are beautiful in God's sight, and no person has a right to suppress anyone else. All through the Old Testament you will find this same truth deeply embedded in what God says to us.

> Have we not all one father? hath not one God created us? why do we deal treacherously every man against his brother? (Mal. 2:10).

There are so many passages in the New Testament:

> God hath made of one blood all nations of men for to dwell on all the face of the earth.

> If God so loved us, we ought to love one another . . .

> Let us not love in word, neither in tongue, but in deed, and in truth.

Divine instruction begins in the first chapter in the Bible, and covers the vast plane of human relationships.

Take the matter of *pollution*. Is there anything in the Bible about it? Turn back to the first chapter in the Book.

> And God blessed them, and God said unto them, Be fruitful, and multiply, and replenish the earth, and subdue it; and have dominion over the fish of the sea, and over the fowl of the air, and over every living thing that moveth upon the earth. And God said, Behold, I have given you

every herb bearing seed, which is upon the face of all the
earth, and every tree, in the which is the fruit of a tree
yielding seed; to you it shall be for meat.

And to every beast of the earth, and to every fowl of
the air, and to every thing that creepeth upon the earth,
wherein there is life, I have given every green herb for
meat: and it was so.

And God saw every thing that he had made, and, behold, it was very good. And the evening and the morning
were the sixth day (1:28–31).

And so God put his creation in our care, to keep it beautiful and
to keep it in balance, instead of polluted and stinking! This duty
began in the first Book, and in the first chapter of the first book
of the Bible.

Let a California Indian tell you what he feels about the white
man as an exploiter:

When we Indians kill meat, we eat it all up. When we
dig roots, we make little holes. . . . We shake down
acorns and pinenuts. We don't chop down trees. We only
use dead wood. But the white people plow up the ground,
pull up the trees, kill everything. The tree says, "Don't.
I am sore. Don't hurt me."

But they chop it down and cut it up . . . The Indians
never hurt anything, but the white people destroy all.
They blast rocks and scatter them on the ground. The rock
says, "Don't! You are hurting me." But the white people
pay no attention.

Everywhere the white man has touched the earth, it is
sore.[1]

God's Word screams at us repeatedly about pollution.

What about *poverty?* Is there anything in the Bible about poverty?

> Pure religion and undefiled before God and the Father
> is this, To visit the fatherless and widows in their affliction,
> and to keep himself unspotted from the world (James
> 1:27).
> Whoso hath this world's good and seeth his brother
> have need, and shutteth up his bowels of compassion from
> him, how dwelleth the love of God in him?
> My little children, let us not love in word, neither in
> tongue; but in deed and in truth (1 John 3:17–18).

What about *sexual morality?* "Thou shalt not commit adultery."
Or turn over to the New Testament, and you will find Jesus saying:
"Ye have heard that it was said by them of old time, Thou shalt
not commit adultery: but I say unto you, That whosoever looketh
on a woman to lust after her hath committed adultery with her
already in his heart" (Matt. 5:27–28). And if you don't think the
Bible has something to say about all of this modern agitation for
legalizing homosexuality, I dare you to read the first chapter of
the book of Romans, and to hear Paul say: "God gave them up—
turned his back on them." And don't think for a moment he won't
do that on our day, too. *How relevant can you get?*

What about *pornography?* Let the Bible speak:

> Abstain from all appearance of evil (1 Thess. 5:22).
> As [a man] thinketh in his heart, so is he (Prov. 23:7).
> But whoso shall offend one of these little ones which
> believe in me, it were better for him that a millstone were
> hanged about his neck, and that he were drowned in the
> depth of the sea (Matt. 18:6).

Now, my friend, that is talking about placing a stumbling block
in front of somebody. That is talking about influence; and that

includes every peddler of filth and pornography—whether on the motion picture screen, or on the printed page! And the person who purchases it and feasts upon it in his own life—the same as the person who peddles it. *How relevant can you get?*

This blessed Book points the way. It's really a light, a guide, that provides us with power for ordering the inner life.

> Thy word have I hid in mine heart, that I might not sin against thee.
> The entrance of thy words giveth light.

This is the proclamation of this Book. It teaches us whither we are bound, and why. It contains the only workable formula on earth for brotherhood, understanding, and peace, and it is God's map that teaches us how to be rid of the burden of sin; and all of us are familiar with sin, because each of us carries his own burden of guilt. But this is God's map, and it stays vital at this point, because it deals with the spiritual world, and it contains the proper information we need in order to find our way in a world of blackness, of darkness, in a world of sin.

If I start out for Niagara Falls and don't already know the way, I'll consult my road map. The road map is very important. It does not become the tumbling waters, nor the beautiful spray, but it is important because it is a precondition for my arriving at Niagara Falls. In this same way, God's Word is a precondition, because of what it says. It is a guide, to lead you and me to the atonement of Jesus Christ, to eternal life, which he provides. It tells us how to trust him and how to be saved:

> If thou shalt confess with thy mouth the Lord Jesus, and shalt believe in thine heart that God hath raised him from the dead, thou shalt be saved (Rom. 10:9).

This is our road map. Relevant? *How relevant can you get!* It is our light and our guide and it beckons you to follow the way that is made very clear to you.

Religion must have a carry-over value. An understanding of the timeless teachings of God's Word will not leave one listless and indifferent. The great imperative laid upon every believer is that he be a "doer of the Word."

MONDAY RELIGION

After a protracted illness, a Christian woman was taken to the hospital for surgery. She was visibly distressed. As she was being prepared for the operation, a Christian attendant took her hand and whispered softly: "Madam, you have nothing to fear. Only one of two things could possibly happen to you, and both of them are good. If you should die, you will be with Jesus; if you should live, Jesus will be with you. In either case, both of you will be together." Could anything be more comforting than that? In health or in sickness, in joy or in sorrow, in life or in death, both of them, Jesus and she, would always be together.

King David, whose life was a constant succession of tragedy and triumph, found strength and assurance in this thought and expressed it in Psalm 139: "How precious also are thy thoughts unto me, O God! . . . When I awake, I am still with thee." This is the Christian's comfort in every dark moment, especially in the dark moments of illness. The night may be long and trying, the sleep fitful and feverish, the body faint, and the heart anxious; but no matter what the trials of the night may be, "when I awake, I am still with thee."

Even after the night of life's little day is over, when the curtains of eternity are lifted, and the sun of righteousness beams forth in all its healing brilliance—even then, in death, "when I awake, I am still with thee." Let us realize, however, that we need not be sick or in trouble or in danger to experience the thrill and the joy of this constant and unbroken companionship every night of our lives, when the toils of the day are done and the lights are turned out and we lay our head upon our pillows to invite sweet rest and slumber. We can close our eyes in the confidence and assurance of this promise. There is nothing in life that can harm us if through faith in Christ, the Savior, we have placed ourselves for time and for eternity securely in the hands of God. His presence will go with us in every circumstance, and in his presence no evil dare come nigh us.

---

[1] *Review & Expositor*, Summer 1970, p. 302.

4.

Preparing for Great Encounters

(1 Samuel 17:27–46)

To be able to participate in the Olympics is for most amateur athletes the greatest honor, and to win a gold medal is the ultimate. One will dream, train, endure demanding preparation for that one great moment. At the starting line he probably feels that everything he has endured and sacrificed has pointed toward that one great moment of truth. He knows that to excell and to win one must be prepared.

Read the details of David's preparation to meet Goliath in deadly combat in 1 Samuel 17:27–46. David, the man after God's own heart; David, the shepherd lad, made thorough and complete preparation to meet his Goliath. If you will look at these smooth stones which David chose for himself, there is a symbolic lesson presented in each of them.

I. THE SMOOTH STONE OF SELF-CONTROL GROWING OUT OF A CONQUERED TEMPER

The first stone is found in verses 28–30. The smooth stone of self-control, which grew out of David's *conquered temper,* became one of the solid stones in his preparation for the job which he must do. Notice here, particularly, the contrast between the irritating taunt of Eliab, his elder brother, and the fine self-possession of David's answer. Temper is a powerful thing; the passion of the spirit is a devastating passion. Nothing on earth disturbs the accuracy of the eye or the steadiness of the hand quite like temper; but David had learned long, long ago to control his temper. He realized that "a soft answer turneth away wrath." He realized that what the New Testament teaches us is a good principle that "we ought to return good for evil." I am sure that many times he had searched his own heart with the probing, prying question of God's Word: "Be angry and sin not?" He realized also that "whom the gods would destroy, they first make mad."

Many people pride themselves on their quick, hot tempers. They say they are temperamental. Somebody has answered that by saying as a normal experience this is about 90 percent temper and about 10 percent mental. Usually when people fly off the handle, it is a sure sign that they have done little thinking and little preparation.

There are some good *pathways to the conquering of one's temper.* (1) Perhaps a person might need a physical examination. When people lose their tempers it is often a sure indication that something has disagreed with them, that they are not well physically, and they need the attention of a good doctor. (2) On the other hand, we can bring to bear our own will power and thus control our tempers. (3) To master it completely, we may bring to bear a good case of Christianity, a good case of religion. I know of no more sure cure for temper than this. "If a man commands you to go one mile, go an extra one with him; if he demands your coat, give him your cloak also." "Turn the other cheek if he smites you on one side." "A soft answer turneth away wrath." "Do good to those who despitefully use you." David had learned his lesson well; he was complete master; he was in absolute control of his temper and he knew how to answer when the moment came that demanded a good answer. So here is the smooth stone of self-control growing out of a conquered temper on the part of David.

II. THE SMOOTH STONE OF QUIET SELF-CONFIDENCE

Another one of the smooth stones is presented in verses 34–37.

Here is the smooth stone of self-confidence based on previous achievements in lesser encounters on the part of David, the man of God. Notice his cool self-confidence as over against the panic not only of his brethren, but of the king and the entire armies of Israel. David seemed to be the only one who had absolute control of himself. How had he developed this attitude?

He had developed this attitude by his faithfulness in lesser encounters all along through his life. Already David is wearing the garlands of victory because he tells us how he had emerged victorious over the lion and the bear. In those crucial experiences on battlefields of lesser magnitude David had been faithful. "He that is faithful in that which is least will be faithful also in that which is much." So now, he is ready for larger undertakings, for greater combat. I love the record of the life of Joseph, one of the very few men in the Bible about whom nothing is said that is contrary to good character. As a matter of fact, Joseph is a type of Christ. All through Joseph's life there was a faithfulness to purity and to his God. He proved himself on the battlefield time after time, so that when the crucial hour of his temptation came, Joseph met it in confidence and in faith. So it is with David in this experience.

Life is little more than a training ground for all of us. We constantly make decisions and fight battles. We go through experiences that fortify and strengthen us, and place us in a position to make greater decisions and accept greater trials and responsibilities. When we are victorious in that which is small, that which is least, then we are ready for our great hour or great moment of destiny.

This is like our experiences in school. Many of you remember the old *Blue Back Speller Book* which you used in school. You will recall that the book began with the simplest words, but as you progressed through the book, day after day, week after week, the words were harder and more difficult to learn, to spell, and to pronounce. This is our experience in the progress of our education and development. When we complete our education on one level, we move on to another. Looking back, we say, "Well, I thought that was hard, but I didn't know anything." On to a different level, we look back and say, "I thought that was difficult, but really I knew nothing." Then eventually when we step out of school and into the professional or business world, we look back upon those school days and say, "Well, I thought I was having a hard time in school, but really, I did not realize what a happy, joyous experience was mine, as I passed along preparing for greater demands that life makes as we live it." This is the process of development, preparation for contests on the battlefield, the track or football field, or the basketball court. Long years of hard training prepare one for the hour of conflict and contest.

Now, this is true about anyone who really prepares himself. The poet has said:

> The heights by great men reached and kept,
>   Were not attained by sudden blight,
> But they, while their companions slept,
>   Were toiling upward in the night.

David had confidence in himself. A person accomplishes very few things in life unless he has confidence in his ability, in his learning and his preparation. Only then is he able to face the critical moment when it comes with quiet confidence like David did. Self-confidence is most important, and the pages of history are literally filled with the records of individuals who accomplish great things when they believed in themselves, to say nothing about those who believed in God. One remembers the record of a young Benjamin Disraeli who, very early in his career, stood before Parliament to make his first speech and was jeered down by Parliament. As he left the floor, he literally shook his fist in the faces of his elders and said to them: "The day will come when you will listen to me." With that kind of confidence he came to be the beloved Prime

Minister under Queen Victoria. Somehow faith or confidence has a way of putting iron into a person's bloodstream, into his very soul. You, as I, might not think much of Henley's theology, but you cannot help but admire his spirit when he says: "It matters not how straight the gate nor how charged with punishment the scroll; I am the master of my fate, I am the captain of my soul." It was Emerson who said: "They can conquer who believe that they can."

I would hasten rapidly to warn against cocksureness, which is not what I am talking about at all. Cocksureness is that kind of overconfidence that grows out of an auto-intoxication based upon an exaggerated sense of one's own importance or his abilities. This is not the kind of confidence that David possessed. There are some of us who need to be taken down a notch or two at this point. We need to have some of the starch knocked out of us. Like the sister and brother in George Kaufman's play, "The President's Daughter": The two stand before a portrait of Grandfather, who had been President of the United States. The brash youth, with his hands in his pockets, said: "I think I can fill his shoes." Disconcerting and deflating, his sister remarked: "It's the other end of grandfather which was most important." Some of us need to have some of this spirit taken out of us. But now, David was a man who had a quiet confidence based upon previous achievements in lesser encounters when he had been faithful to himself and to his God.

III. THE SMOOTH STONE OF FRANK ACCEPTANCE OF OURSELVES

In verses 38–40 we find *the smooth stone of frank acceptance of himself.* Confidence in himself and his own preparation, depending not upon someone else for success in life, David threw off Saul's armour which well-wishing but unwise friends put upon him. You remember who Saul was? He was the king of Israel. Do you remember about his selection? When the prophet of God came to find him, the Bible tells us that he was "head and shoulders above all his contemporaries." Saul was a giant of a man. Now, think about the armour that he must have had, the size sword and shield. Here is a strippling shepherd boy from the open hills. He puts on the heavy armour that was entirely too large for him in the first place, and "he assayed to go forth," which to me indicates that he probably wobbled and struggled under the weight as well as the size of the armour. What a tragic mistake when people endeavor to live like others and expect themselves to measure up to the exact specifications of their fellow man. Every principle in God's Word indicates to us that each of us is endowed with his own ability, with his own talents, and is commanded to use them and not to begrudge the other fellow of his abilities, of his talents. David preferred to meet Goliath with the equipment and the skill that he himself had mastered.

It is probably the experience of every young preacher boy, after hearing others preach awhile, to pick out an ideal and want to be like that older person who has experience and background, and perhaps ability. I was no exception. I had several along the way. One of them was Dr. George W. Truett; I had heard him a few times when I was a small lad. I have never in my life heard a man who could preach like George W. Truett. I wanted to be like him. There were others along the way. Then one day I came to the conclusion that when I attempted to mimic or copy another person, then that person certainly was not there because I did not have the ability that he had, nor was I there because I was making a pretense at an ability which I did not possess. So I decided that my talents, as weak as they might be, were talents that God evidently felt that he needed, that I was to be to God all that I could be in my own abilities and not try to mimic or copy another person. This was the feeling of this young man, David.

Accepting oneself as he is does not mean being satisfied. I do not believe that David ever was really satisfied with himself. When you become satisfied with your abilities or with your possessions, then,

I think, you are ready for the retirement center or perhaps the graveyard. There is a vast difference between being content and being satisfied. Paul said: "I have learned in whatsoever state I am, therewith [not to be satisfied] to be content." Paul stated repeatedly that he was ever struggling on and up to try to lay hold upon that for which God had laid hold upon him. So David wanted to be a success for the glory of God. He took what he had and used it to maximum advantage.

A few years ago my heart was thrilled, as I am sure yours was if you remember the incident, when the State Athletic Gymnastic Contest for Arizona was held. One of the men who excelled (he came in fourth in the entire state in overall ability) was a young man with one leg. Here was a man who refused to let life and its handicaps get him down, a man who was willing to accept himself as he was and then to use his talents to the very best of his ability. Thank God for people who use their talents and their abilities.

One secret of success in Andrew Jackson's life is told by a boyhood friend who said: "I could throw him three times out of four but he would never stay throwed." Jackson, an unschooled orphan, became one of our greatest leaders, a man of tremendous ability: Handicaps became stepping stones to him.

IV. THE SMOOTH STONE OF UNSELFISH DEVOTION TO SOMETHING BEYOND SELF

Verses 26 and 29 describe the smooth stone of unselfish devotion to something beyond himself. The chances are, had David looked at himself and thought about his own physical handicaps, his size in comparison with Goliath, and all of the other selfish interests that he might have had at stake, that he would not have had the nerve or the courage to face the giant. Instead, he looked beyond himself and saw that there was a need and a cause, because the armies of Israel as well as Israel's God had been defied by this pagan giant. So David answered his elder brother, Eliab: "Is there not a cause" that calls for one's life as well as one's ability? David answered and responded to the call.

There are two kinds of winged insects that love to visit gardens. One, beautifully garbed in a coat of iridescent colors, flops on flower, leaf, or stem and continues to eat it until it is utterly destroyed. This is the Japanese bettle. The other insect has a fuzzy, brown coat. It flies from flower to flower gathering nectars and pollens. It does more than take away; it carries from one flower to another the different pollens so necessary for the strength and beauty of the next generation. This insect is called the honey bee, always giving as well as earning his own livelihood. There is a vast amount of difference between the two insects!

There are some people who are like Japanese beetles in their experience. All on earth they know how to do is to receive, to devour, to destroy—everything is built around and for them. On the other hand there are people who are like the honey bees. They not only earn their own livelihood, but they serve their generation and their God well because they believe there is a cause.

One of the highlights of the annual session of the Southern Baptist Convention is Foreign Mission night. It is inspiring to realize that so many respond to God's call to help meet the over-whelming needs of mankind. Is there not a cause? This is the smooth stone of unselfish devotion to something beyond self.

V. THE SMOOTH STONE OF FAITH IN GOD— ASSURANCE OF HELP FROM HIM

There is a fifth stone, and you will find it referred to in verses 37, 45–47. This is the smooth stone of faith in God and assurance of help from him at the right time. Is not "the battle the Lord's?" Out of a lifetime of experience, David could come to the end of the way and say:

The Lord is my shepherd; I shall not want. He maketh

me to lie down in green pastures: he leadeth me beside the still waters. He restoreth my soul: he leadeth me in the paths of righteousness for his name's sake. Yea, though I walk through the valley of the shadow of death, I will fear no evil: for thou art with me; thy rod and thy staff they comfort me. Thou preparest a table before me in the presence of mine enemies: thou anointest my head with oil; my cup runneth over. Surely goodness and mercy shall follow me all the days of my life: and I will dwell in the house of the Lord for ever" (Ps. 23).

Because God led, guided, and protected all through David's life, he knew when he met Goliath that he was sufficient. You and I can be just as confident as we meet the Goliaths of our own experience and our own lives with a deep and profound faith in God. We cannot fail.

Many years ago in the Scottish highlands there was a botanist looking for unusual wild flowers. The story is told that he came to one precipitous area. Looking over the side he spotted a brilliant flower, way down on the side of the cliff. He did not know how on earth he could get it. Finally, he spotted a young shepherd boy and called to him, offering to pay him if he would go down and get the flower. He offered to hold the rope to let the boy over the cliff and down where the flower was growing. The boy said, "Wait a minute." He disappeared into the woods and in a little while came back with his own father. Then he said to the botanist: "I will get your flower, providing my own father holds the end of the rope." You and I can go over the side of any precipice, we can face any Goliath, we can go through any suffering, we can accomplish anything to which we set our hands, heads, and hearts *providing* our heavenly Father holds the other end of the rope. You know, David had the assurance in his heart that God was sufficient!

Adequate preparation in life for any undertaking reaches its climax in a deep awareness of God's presence and power in life.

Any person, like David, who is willing to pay the price can have such assurance.

THE GIANTS OF LIFE

Every person who knows anything at all about the Bible is well acquainted with the familiar record of how the young Hebrew champion, David, defeated the Philistine giant, Goliath. Goliath came out repeatedly and called out to the armies of Israel, "I defy the armies of Israel this day. Give me a man, that we may fight together. Send out your champion to fight me, and let the winner be the victor of the war," and his voice rang out like a peal of thunder. The giant was no ordinary man. He was of such an enormous size and so completely armed that the sight of him brought terror to the Israelite camp.

No one of us can ignore the fact that we today face giants. The giant of communism has been roaring and breathing threatenings for twenty years and as yet there is no solution to the problem. Its tremendous ideology has swept over the world and kept the world on the defensive.

Likewise, we face the giant of nuclear power that could destroy our civilization. The world we live in today is the most terrifying world that any group of people ever faced. Add to these giants the awful face of moral deterioration in our nation, the complicated problems of racial differences, the giant of sexual promiscuity, etc., and we begin to see something of the tremendous forces present in our world against which we must battle.

It is high time that all of us realize that, like young David, we cannot win the battle by ourselves. We must have the help of God. In fact, we hardly know how to handle these giants. We have been defeated so often that it is difficult to find the courage to continue battling against them. David saw and heard Goliath and knew immediately in his heart that he must go out and face that giant. The motivating power that sent him forth was the presence of the spirit of God speaking to his heart and his assurance that God would give him the victory.

The story indicates clearly that God was with him in the hour of trial. When the stone left his sling, it struck the giant on the forehead. Goliath stood for a second dazed and shaken, and then toppled to the ground. David ran, lifted the giant's sword, cut off his head, and the Philistine troops began running. Israel won a great battle that day because one young man had given his life without reservation to God. Such devotion and dedication as David possessed, when it is placed in the hands of an all powerful God, will always win the victory for him. Later David said in one of his beautiful psalms, "Call upon me in the day of trouble, and I will deliver thee, and thou shalt glorify me."

THE SUFFERING OF GOD'S CHILDREN

"Every branch that beareth fruit, he purgeth it, that it may bring forth more fruit" (John 15:2).

To any farmer, gardener, or citrus man, the term "pruning" immediately rings a bell. Both the process and purpose are clearly understood. When done at the right time, marvelous transformation can take place and the plant begins to produce in abundance. A recent article admonished, "Now is the time to prune your poinsettias, if you expect them to be at their best by Christmas time."

Our heavenly Father sometimes finds it necessary to "cut back" the plants that are growing in his garden. We Christians might be likened to trees—planted, cultivated, and nurtured by the miracle of his grace. In the process of growth it is essential for pruning to be done on the branches that are bearing fruit—that they might bring forth more fruit. The brittle brush and useless twigs must constantly be cut away to assure and to multiply the yield of the plant. This process is necessary even though painful and unpleasant.

Most all people who suffer are plagued at one time or another with the problem of why God's children must often suffer. Why is it that devoted and pious Christians, men and women who strive with all their hearts to conform their lives to the will of Christ, seem to suffer one disappointment after another? Of course the complete answer to that question will never be given this side of heaven. The Bible tells us that here on this earth we "see through a glass darkly—but then face to face." God has revealed, however, just enough of his design to which we can pin our faith. He tells us in John 15:12: "Every branch that beareth fruit, he purgeth it, that it may bring forth more fruit." In other words, the Christian is to be better, more fruitful as a result of the "cut back." Look at the life of the apostle Paul. In 2 Corinthians 11, he lays bare his breast, and displays the countless scars of the pruning hook of God's unsearchable providence. He tells us that he was "beaten with rods, stoned, in perils in the sea, in hunger and thirst, in cold and nakedness." Yet, no one will deny that the life of this great man of God was more fruitful because of these painful visitations. Many of you have gone through similar experiences. God has found it necessary to "cut back" drastically some branch in your life on which you had pinned your highest hopes. Perhaps your "cut back" has amounted to the loss of health, wealth, a beloved son or daughter, or some bitter disillusionment. These are painful cut backs, to be sure, but they can be cut backs with a gracious purpose. Please remember that when the days of pruning come,

God is not cutting down the tree. He is rather improving one of its branches. He is preparing it for greater fruitfulness.

SILENCE

"Be still, and know that I am God" (Ps. 46:10).

There is nothing so impressive as silence. The most musical voices of nature can be heard only when man himself is still. It is then that "she speaks a varied language." High up on the mountainside, where the Potomac and the Shenandoah mingle their floods to roll together toward the sea, there is a tilting rock known as Jefferson's Rock. According to tradition, it was when he was standing on that rock that Jefferson received inspiration for the description of that grand and beautiful country in his "Notes on Virginia." For beneath, toward the south and east, the beautiful Shenandoah flows over shelves of rock. The waters make noble music; but if you are speaking on the rock, you cannot hear that music. It is only when you are still that you hear the voice of the river.

All of nature speaks thus through silence. The sea is magnificent when it is broken and driven by the lash of the wind, but it is still grander and more mysterious when it lies under your ship without a wave, motionless, as a sea of glass. The mountains are noble in their silence, and so is the forest when not a leaf stirs beneath the wind. It is never when the hunter or woodsman is crashing through the undergrowth, with the leaves and the fallen branches breaking beneath his feet, that he hears what the forest has to say; it is only when he leans his gun against a tree and sits down on a fallen log, then he can hear the voice of the forest—the grinding of one limb against another, the fall of a nut, the flitting of wings, the scamper of a rabbit, the drumming of the woodpecker, and the tops of the trees, the gentle stirring of the wind, like the sigh of a soul that has found its peace. It seems that the forest says: "Be still, and you will hear my voice."

Why cannot we take a lesson from the voices of nature and realize that the deeper things of life can be fully heard and appreciated only as we give time and attention to the development of the spirit.

UNSELFISHNESS

A wealthy man had no sons but did have three nephews. He wished very much to leave the main responsibility of his business to the boy who was most capable of carrying it on. One day he called all three of them unto his office and said to them: "One of you will be my successor. I shall give you each a coin. This large room must be filled with something purchased with the coin. You must fill the room as full as you can, but spend no more money than this amount. Return this evening and I shall be waiting." The boys thanked him for his trust in them, and then departed their separate ways and made their purchases.

When evening came, the boys returned and the man was awaiting them. The first youth had bought two huge bales of straw, which filled half of the room. The second youth had bought two bags of thistle-down which, when released, flew everywhere, but when it had settled filled only three-fourths of the room. The third lad stood sadly by. His uncle inquired, "And what did you purchase, son?" He answered, "I gave half of my coin to feed a hungry child, most of the rest of it I gave to the church where I knelt to pray. Then with the few cents I had left, I purchased these matches and a tall candle." With these words he lit the candle, and the light filled every corner of the room. The old man smiled and said approvingly to the third lad, "You alone have caused the room to be filled." The young man fell to his knees as the old man blessed him and made him his successor.

One of the great principles of the Bible and one of the strongest virtues of Christianity is that of unselfishness. The Christian religion teaches us that a person truly finds his life only when he loses it in service and ministry to God and to mankind. May I leave this little prayer by an unknown author in your heart today?

Dear God, the light has come, our outgrown creeds
Drop from us as a garment, and our sight
Grows clearer to see ourselves and Thee aright;
We trust your love to meet our utmost needs,
And know Thy hand sustains us.
The foul deeds
Of nameless doubts and fears that thronged the night
Like phantoms disappear in truth's clear light;
Self only, now our upward way impedes;
For thou hast given new bottles for truth's wine;
Hast given a larger faith to help us live
A larger life; new knowledge that will give
A lamp to lead us on to the divine:
And though our feet may falter in the way,
Yet shall our eyes behold love's perfect day!

5.

Sins of Omission

(Joshua 11:15)

"As the Lord commanded Moses his servant, so did Moses command Joshua, and so did Joshua; he left nothing undone of all that the Lord commanded Moses." Isn't that a marvelous statement!

The circumstances involved were these: Moses went up to the top of Mount Nebo, where he met God. On top of lonely Nebo he died, and the Lord buried his body. Israel was stripped of her leader, the one who had led her out of Egyptian bondage, and the mantle of Moses fell upon Joshua, his lieutenant. Joshua was responsible to God for the commandments God gave to Moses, his predecessor. The conquest of Canaan was before them. Joshua carried out the instructions which the Lord gave for the accomplishment of the task, and settlement in the Land of Promise.

When you read the larger context of our Scripture you find many details involved in these instructions. For instance, "Joshua smote all the country of the hills and of the south and of the vales and of the springs and all of their kings. He left nothing remaining but thoroughly destroyed all that breathed as the Lord God of Israel commanded that he should do." And again, "Joshua did unto them as the Lord bade him. He hocked their horses and burned their chariots with fire." Then verse 15 tells us that in obedience, in faithfulness, Joshua carried out all the things that God had commanded. How marvelous to come to the end of the battle, how wonderful to come to the end of a life, how thrilling for one to be able to look back upon the past, and to sit down in confidence and faith and say as Paul says, "I have fought a good fight, I have finished my course, I have kept the faith: henceforth there is laid up for me a crown of righteousness, which the Lord, the righteous judge, shall give me at that day." Joshua did everything that God commanded and he left nothing undone!

How blessed and fortunate is the individual who can say, "I have left nothing undone of all that God commanded from the beginning." However, I am afraid that very few can honestly make such a claim.

Andrew Bonar, the great Christian preacher of another age, said one day as he came to the end of a year in his life, "This year omissions distressed me more than anything." A great artist painted a picture of the Lord's Supper and presented it to Tolstoi. He studied it for a moment and then, turning to his friend the artist, he said: "Sir, you do not love this one very much! If you had loved him more, you would have painted him better."

As a child I heard my mother pray many, many times, at the table, on her knees, in the bed, and many other places. I do not recall but few times when I heard her that somewhere in her prayer she did not utter a petition something like this: "O Lord, forgive us our sins of omission as well as our sins of commission." That is a heart-searching petition and prayer and one that all of us need to pray. Our chief concern in this message is with our disobedience in activity, in our responsibilities unto the Lord. We are not primarily concerned with what we purposed, or intended, or planned to do. What we are concerned about are those supreme things that God commanded us to do which we have left off. These are the things that should cause us great concern.

I. SINS OF OMISSION ARE TOO NUMEROUS TO LIST

Like Andrew Bonar, as we view the past, I am sure that in the mind and heart of each of us there looms very large the fact that so much should have been done that we failed to do. When you begin thinking about the things undone, they become so numerous that they pile up mountainous high; and it would seem that we omitted much more than we actually did or accomplished. We think we are busy. We love to talk about how much we do in a day or how much we do in a week, or a month or a year. We talk about our schedules and how busy we are. Most of us are busy— too busy for our own good!

Mr. Howard Butt, prominent Baptist layman from Texas, says that modern man thinks he is much busier than he actually is. He said that our forefathers years ago could miss a wagon train going west and sit down and wait for a week on another one without thinking anything about it; today, if we miss one section of a revolving door we develop a stomach ulcer as a result. He also said that one fellow came up with this ear-catcher: "You know, the hurry-ier I get the behinder I am!" Isn't that true with most of us? We are entirely too busy with the things that we do and that we plan to do. On the other hand, if all of a sudden the multitudinous things that we fail to do should loom out of the past we would be surprised and overwhelmed at their number.

In 1 Kings 20 there is a marvelous statement along this line in the Old Testament parable of the Lost Prisoner. These were the circumstances: Benhadad, the king of Syria, made war against Ahab, the king of Israel, and was soundly defeated; but Ahab failed to do what God told him to do about destroying the Syrians—Benhadad in particular—and let them go. One of the prophets of God disguised himself one day and sat on the roadside when Ahab came by. He told him a parable about a guard who had entrusted to him a prisoner. The point of the whole story was this. The prophet said to Ahab: "As thy servant was busy here and there, behold he was gone." I submit to you that that is true about so many things in our lives. As thy servant became so involved, so busy here and there, behold the prisoners of opportunity were flown.

Things undone loom mountainous high in the period of youth. Actually, the whole of life is one golden prisoner committed into our hands for a day and for the opportunities the day brings.

Young people need to realize that in this time of life there must be some things decided, some goal lines crossed, some ideals established, some attainments realized. There must be preparation of mind, body, and soul, else the prisoner of opportunity flee, and we never will be able to recapture him.

When a farmer fails to get out in March and April with his plow and break the ground and sow the seed and cultivate the plants, he will starve when December comes. When the pools of life are stirred by the angel of God, then we must step down into the water, because it is then or never as far as we are concerned. You might go out on a spring morning and look at the beautiful roses sparkling with a thousand diamonds of glory in the early morning dew. You must realize that in a few moments of time the dew is gone. You can go out at the noon-day hour and pour water for an hour or more over the bushes, but you will be utterly incapable of recapturing the beauty and the glory of the morning dew. The same is true of the freshness of youth. The poet has expressed it in these words:

> Break, break, break at the foot of thy crags, O Sea!
> But the tender grace of a day that is dead
> Will never come back to me.

Maybe that is the reason that Solomon in Ecclesiastes says: "Rejoice, O young man, in thy youth; and let thy heart cheer thee in the days of thy youth, and walk in the ways of thine heart, and in the sight of thine eyes: but know thou, that for all these things God will bring thee into judgment." "While thy servant was busy here and there, behold he was gone." Suddenly youth is gone, and many fail to make of life what it ought to be.

Look at the home circle for a moment. How negligently we deal with our loved ones who are so near and dear to our hearts, until change or death removes them from our grasp. The disciples who were with the Master in the garden of Gethsemane were sound asleep in the golden hour of their opportunity. Jesus came and said:

"What, could ye not watch with me just one hour?" One hour of
service, one hour of opportunity, and then the prisoner was gone;
and no more the chances, no more the opportunities were presented unto them. And in the home we are often sound asleep. We
neglect, we omit doing those things that mean so much to the
hearts of those we love. If you have an impulse in your heart to
say something, to do something, to be something, I admonish in
the name of Jesus Christ to say it, to do it, and to be it NOW, before
the prisoner is gone and you look back with sorrow saying, "Oh,
if only I had—when the opportunity was mine!"

> I did not know how short your day would be!
> I had you safe, and words could wait awhile—
> E'en when your eyes begged tenderness of me,
> Behind their smile.
> And now for you, so dark, so long, is night!
> I speak, but on my knees, unheard, alone—
> What words were these to make a short day
>   bright—If I had known!
> Ah, love—if I had known!

How often loved ones lament as they look back, "Oh, did I do
everything I should have done, did I say everything I should have
said when the opportunities were there?" Squire was the one who
wrote a poem in which he pictured a man who always had good
intentions where his loved ones were concerned. Every day he
decided he was going to write to this loved one but he failed to
do it. He said, "Tomorrow I will do it." But his tomorrow had
a way of stretching out into eternities, always intending, but so
absorbed in duties that he neglected it. One day the letter came.
She was dead. He clutched the letter, then looked again at the
words in his hands, and in a flood of remorse that rushes upon him
he cried: "It shall not be today. It shall not! It is still yesterday.
There is still time—there must be time!" Poor unhappy soul!

The sun moves. Our outward course is set.
There will be time for nothing but regret,
And the memory of things undone!

J. P. Marquand has captured this idea and put it into a book entitled *So Little Time*. The story concerns a playwright who has good intentions and purposes about writing a masterpiece and about being a real father and husband in his home. Finally his oldest son puts on a uniform and goes off to war. The man realizes that maybe life is all too brief for his boy, and sets about trying to repair the damage and trying to do some of the things that he had neglected to do all of these years while he was in the home with his boy. Over and over again there is that tragic lament, the refrain which is the title of the book, "So little time, so little time!" Oh, in the family circle there are so many things that are undone!

Out in the wider reaches of the community where we rub shoulders with people, think of the words that could have been spoken, think of the handclasps that could have meant encouragement and comfort to somebody. Think of the appreciation you could have shown to someone else, but these things have been left undone. The real ghosts of human life are the unwritten letters, the unspoken words, the unmade visits, the little things that we let slip by us day in and day out.

Then there is the work of God, of the Kingdom, and of the church; how we fail in these! Think of the times when we could have given more, when we could have talked, when we could have witnessed. Here is one of the great contrasts between the vast world of nature and human life. Have you ever stopped to think that in nature practically everything fulfills its purpose, if let alone, just exactly as God intended it? God set it here for a purpose, and with what energy it pursues its purpose! But in human life all too often we are paralyzed with inertia, laziness, procrastination, fear, balking at the task and the job. So these things loom mountainous high—the things that we leave undone that should have been done.

II. SINS OF OMISSION IMPORTANT

The things that we leave undone so often are the most important matters in life.

Did you ever hear the story about the country boy who never had seen a circus? One came to the county seat town one day, so his father called him and gave him a silver dollar and sent him to the circus. When the lad arrived, the parade was in progress, coming right down Main Street. He made his way into the crowd that had gathered; he watched the horses that came by, he watched the elephants, and was fascinated by the lions and tigers in their cages. As he watched the clowns cavorting, one of them came close to him with his hand outstretched. The boy said, "This is it." He pulled the silver dollar out of his pocket and dropped it into the hand of the clown, and went his way back home. Not until weeks later did he realize that he had missed the circus, and the only thing that he had seen was just the parade, the preliminaries. All too often in life that is exactly what we do.

Emerson spoke about there being a "science of omitting." In a day when there are conflicting interests, philosophies clamoring for our obedience, countless things pulling at us for our love and loyalty, if we do not learn how to omit, God have mercy upon us. On the moral plane, life becomes successful only as we learn to exclude.

Schiller says, "The artist may be known rather by what he omits." That is also true about the orator and about the literary genius. After all, they become known by what they omit. You cannot include everything in life. They know how to omit the vulgar, the incidental, the irrelevant, and major upon the main things. You have learned how to omit some things, to exclude some things. To know when and how to omit is a fine art.

The artist William Hunt once had a class of students on a hillside, painting the sunset. He walked from person to person, looking over the shoulders of the students as they labored over their canvasses until he came to one fellow who meticulously painted the shingles on an old barn that stood out on the hillside. The great artist tapped him on the shoulder and said, "Son, if you waste so much time with the shingles of that old barn you'll never get to the sunset before it is too late." Isn't that true of most of us? We haven't mastered the art of selecting, of omitting, of excluding some things and majoring upon others. Therefore, this is our indictment—what miserable artists we are, because we include so many irrelevant things and then we fail to magnify the supremely important things. Consider one or two of these things.

For instance, look at the vast area of character building. Incidentally, Jesus had a word for that in Matthew 23:23. We often quote this passage in talking about tithing, and it is very appropriate, but it has something else to say too. "Woe unto you, scribes and Pharisees, hypocrites! for ye pay tithes of mint and anise and cummin [now here is the point], and have omitted the weightier matters of the law, judgment, mercy, and faith. These ought ye to have done, and not to leave the other undone." So often we major upon minors and omit the eternal things, the things that are worthwhile in the building of character which must stand when the world has disintegrated and disappeared.

Then there is the area of duty in our relationship to the eternal. On the spiritual plane, how easy it is to leave the most important things undone. How easy it is for people to postpone making a decision for Jesus Christ and for church membership. We all meet them regularly. An unsaved person might have good intentions about trusting in Christ, but he drifts along; he finds it so easy to continue to put it off. Or, here is a person who lives in a community for a month, six months, a year, ten years, twenty years, unaffiliated with God's church and with God's people, always having good intentions, but just omitting things that are really worthwhile. Jeremiah, talking about a period of time when the nations went to war with each other, said, "The harvest is past, the summer is ended, and we are not saved!" This is appropriate for the end of a time of revival when many people have failed to respond to God's invitation. It is also appropriate when you come to the end of a year and do some stock-taking. In view of failures it is very appropriate to say, "The summer is ended, the harvest is past, and I am not saved. I haven't done what God wanted me to do with my soul, with my life." The writer of the book of Hebrews says, "How shall we escape if we neglect so great salvation!" Yet many have a way of putting off, of neglecting it. These are really the most important things. Usually the things that we leave undone are the most important things in the long run.

III. ULTIMATE RESPONSIBILITY FOR SINS OF OMISSION

There is a further timely word about this matter. We are held accountable, responsible to God for sins of omission, just as for sins of commission. We ultimately are responsible for things undone. For instance, they have a way of rising up out of the tombs of time to mock and condemn.

Several years ago Dr. Courts Redford, Executive Secretary of the Home Mission Board of the Southern Baptist Convention, wrote an article dealing with the opportunities for Christian missions and what happens when people do not grasp those opportunities.[2] He used several illustrations. For instance, have you ever wondered what might have happened if the early churches in North Africa (and, after all, some of the strongest churches in the world in the first two or three centuries were in North Africa) had been concerned primarily about evangelism and missions and Christian education instead of jockeying for positions politically and ecclesiastically? What would be the condition of Africa today? The chances are that all of Africa would be genuinely Christian if only those first churches had been on the job as they should have been. The tragedy is that they have omitted doing the important things.

Then in the thirteenth century Kublai, the king of the Tartans in the Far East, sent a message to the Pope in Rome begging for one hundred missionaries to be sent to the Orient for the purpose of teaching them the way of Christ, bringing Christianity and salvation to the people of the Orient. But the papacy was too busy to listen to the call. The papacy was bent upon a program of self-emulation, of political prestige and power. So the Pope sent two missionaries, who started their journey and never did complete it. They turned around and went back home, and didn't pay any attention to the call of Kublai, the king of the Tartans. What if the church had answered the call? China, Japan, Korea and other areas of the Far East probably today would be genuinely Christian and sending missionaries to the other parts of the world.

In the latter part of the eighteenth century, 1894, there was a young man by the name of Stalin, who, believe it or not, enrolled at the Tiflis Theological Seminary as a student to study for the priesthood. What might have happened if that seminary had put into his fiery bosom an evangelistic zeal and a love for Christ, instead of smothering his initiative and endeavoring to make his life over in a way that was neither Christian nor social? He probably would have come out of the seminary an honor graduate and gone out as herald of the gospel of Christ. Who knows? Maybe the whole course of present-day history would have been changed completely. Surely the things we fail to do have a way of looming up out of the past to mock and condemn us. Just as surely as we live, we are held responsible for the negative as well as the positive. The parable of the Talents bears that out. One man received one talent, but he was afraid. He went and hid it in the earth, and then when the appointed time came he dug it up and gave it to the master of the vineyard. The master of the vineyard said to him: "Thou wicked and slothful servant." He was not wicked in the sense that he had misused his lord's money. It was simply that he failed to use it as he should have.

When the Son of man comes in his glory and all the holy angels with him, we are told that the nations of the earth will be gathered before him, and he will push some to the left, saying unto them, "Inasmuch as ye did it not to one of the least of these, ye did it not to me." Things undone will be a principle of divine judgment. In the parable of the good Samaritan, the priest and the Levite passed the man by on the other side of the road. Wherein was their condemnation? They did not rob him; they just simply withheld from him something that he needed. It was what they failed to do that drew the condemnation of a just and righteous God.

What can we do about it? We can look in penitence into the past and pray God's forgiveness for these things left undone that should have been done. God has a way of being gracious and merciful to us when we do that. We can pray as did Archbishop Ussher in his last words spoken upon his deathbed, when he said, "Lord, forgive my sins, especially my sins of omission." Or, as the Litany expresses it: "That it may please Thee to give us true repentance; to forgive us all our sins, negligences and ignorances!" Or, as the psalmist expresses it in Psalm 19:12, "Who can understand his errors? cleanse thou me from secret faults."

Then we can turn and face the future with hope and confidence. When our hearts are right with God and God's purposes dwell within us, and we have determination to live as he wants us to live, then we have assurance from him that each new year will bring a fresh and new opportunity. Like the poet has expressed it:

> He came to my desk with quivering lip—
> The lesson was done.
> "Dear teacher, I want a new leaf" he said,
> "I've spoiled this one."
>
> I took the old leaf, stained and blotted,
> And gave him a new one all unspotted,
> And into his sad eyes smiled
> "Do better now, my child."

That is exactly what God does! The Lord says to the Philadelphian church, "I set before you an open door which no man can shut." Paul in Philippians makes this remark: "Forgetting those things which are behind, and reaching forth unto those things which are before, I press toward the mark for the prize of the high calling of God in Christ Jesus."

With renewed zeal, let each of us grasp every golden opportunity of service and fellowship to God and our fellowman.

STRENGTH IN FELLOWSHIP

"Comfort yourselves together . . ." (1 Thess. 5:11).

As the result of a severe rain and windstorm, a good many trees in a lovely residential area were uprooted and considerable other damage done. In a little park at the center of the city, a beautiful tree had suffered severely from the wind, but, because of the other trees all about which offered support, it had not gone completely down. Tree surgeons came to its rescue, straightened it up, supported it with cables and braces, and in the course of a year or two, it sent new roots down into the ground, took a new grip on the earth, and is now flourishing again.

Only the eternal God can know how many people would have gone down under discouragement and failure if it had not been for the strength furnished them by their associates—others who were not so badly shaken by the storm. In no other respect does the church of Christ furnish more ample justification for its existence than at this very point—brotherhood. A middle-aged man started on the long, hard road back to security and independence made this remark: "It has been my friends in the church that have kept me going the last two years." Certainly the sermons helped, the preacher inspired, but it was "the brethren" who had given him the courage to make the new effort toward self-respect. The church which does not furnish such fellowship to its members is not functioning as a Christian church. People who have never studied a Bible concordance would probably be amazed at the number of times the work "brethren" appears in the New Testament. Very few words appear on the lips of the apostle Paul so frequently as this one.

Who among us can tell how many people have been held back from contemplated sin and surrender to temptation through the thought of the "fellowship" in one's church, civic club, fraternal organization, and community. It is entirely possible for a person to be a Christian and yet remain outside the church, but the man who attempts to do so is cutting himself off from a source of strength and courage that may be invaluable to him in the hour of crisis. In this fellowship people have come together because of a common experience they have enjoyed and the fellowship in which they now walk with the Lord. It is not composed of people who think they are perfect, but of people who have found a perfect ideal in Christ and are undertaking, more or less successfully, to follow after that ideal. The arms of the church are wide open and the invitation extended: "Comfort yourselves together."

---

[1] James S. Stewart, *The Gates of New Life* (New York: Scribner's, 1940), p. 226.
[2] Courts, Redford, *Home Missions Magazine,* Mar. 1956.

6.

Learning from a Successful Failure

(2 Samuel 18:18–33)

Two scenes are pictured in this passage—the battlefield and the anxious vigil of the king by the wall.

First, look at the battlefield. The forces of King David and those of his rebellious son, Absalom, are locked in deadly combat. We behold the tragic end of Absalom and his restless intrigues, his unbridled passions, and his dazzling hopes. His broken, bleeding body is thrown like a carcass of a dog into the pit and mercilessly covered with stones. In verse 18, the writer tells us that Absalom wanted above all things to be remembered. He designed for himself a burial place "in the king's dale," but what a remembrance he actually has! His crude grave preaches anew the vanity of vaulting ambitions which o'erleaps itself and tells us that:

> Only the actions of the just
> Smell sweet, and blossom in the dust.

The other scene presented is that of King David standing by the wall anxiously awaiting some word from the battlefield. When the messenger delivered the sad news, David "went up to the chamber over the gate, and wept: and as he went, thus he said, O my son Absalom, my son, my son Absalom! would God I had died for thee, O Absalom, my son, my son!" This is an exceeding bitter cry. After all these years it still makes the human blood run cold. Many centuries have come and gone, but David's tears have not been dried by the flight of summer suns. Who is this man in abandoned grief? It is of great significance to remember that he is a father,

71

not a mother, now appearing in the role of just a plain father breaking his heart over what he considers to be the greatest failure of his life! His sensitive poet-nature probably felt the emotions all the keener.

I. DAVID PRESENTS A STRANGE COMBINATION OF SUCCESS AND FAILURE

David was vastly successful. One could well imagine him occupying the hero role in one of Horatio Alger's stories. He had come up from the ranks, a shepherd lad of humble origin and family background. He possessed a mind as brilliant as the sunlight dancing upon the clear waters of a lake. He was dauntless in courage, and will ever remain a hero to youthful hearts. He possessed the genius of a poet, and wrote some of the most magnificent sections contained in the Word of God. In his spiritual development, he reached the proportions of a great saint. In every detail of his life, he was vastly attractive, with the exception of the one great sin which he committed against God. When you read the record of his life, you cannot help but feel that David cast a spell upon all of his contemporaries and left a long shadow that still appears on the horizon.

David made good as a king by right of his ability, and not simply because he was the popular choice of the people. He proved himself to be a great statesman and a great soldier and served his people well as the second king of the United Kingdom of Israel. Israel as a nation became strong and influential. The period of David's reign has often been referred to as the "golden age of Israel." In our day, the story of David's life would be the best subject imaginable for the popular television program, "This Is Your Life," or he would become the central character in a best-selling novel. Yes, indeed, David was successful.

Just as every coin has two sides, so does David's life. Now turn the coin and see the one word written across the back side—FAIL-

URE. David a failure? In what? As a father! Our passage reveals the result of this failure. The body of his handsome, gifted, and brilliant son lies crushed in a pit under a pile of rocks. David's brilliancy of success in one area magnifies his failure in the other. His success, like that of multitudes of fathers in our day, was bought at too high a price. He was guilty of the age-old sin of majoring on minors and minoring on majors. Now hear him cry: "My son, my son."

In the combination of success and failure, we have a perfect picture of a tragedy repeated time without number. A man will become an amazing success in the financial and business world, and even stand on the topmost pinnacle in the social whirl. He possesses a keen mind and marvelous business acumen. He drives himself day and night in order to make a name and build a business or an estate. He becomes successful. In the process, he neglects his children, shows no discipline, indulges them in their every whim and fancy. The day finally comes when tragedy strikes and the man is dazed with the realization that he has spent all of his time making a living for his family, but that he has done absolutely nothing in helping his children make a life for themselves. In this department he is a failure!

II. A FATHER FILLED WITH GRIEF

As we read this scriptural record, the question immediately arises: "Why is David so heart-broken?" The answer is threefold.

(1) David loved Absalom. This is most significant because fathers are not generally credited with doing much loving where children are concerned. This is both unfortunate and unfair. To realize how true this is, simply contrast the celebration of Mother's Day with that of Father's Day. Mother's Day somehow appeals to every deep emotion of the heart. Of course handkerchiefs are in evidence on both days—on Mother's Day to dry our tears, and on Father's Day to stifle our yawns. The common sentiment is that

we must have a day on which to honor our fathers because "every dog has his day." In spite of all of this, observance of Father's Day is timely and necessary, not so much from the point of view of honoring our fathers as showing a little appreciation for them and challenging them to be better fathers than they are. David's heart is broken over his boy.

(2) David is grieved because of the utter finality of the tragedy. In the experience of every human being, there are some mistakes made that can be corrected and God is gracious enough to give a second chance. However, in many instances, there is no next time. For instance, there is no second time for a boy to grow up. There is no next time for parents to be wise in rearing their children. The writer of the book of Hebrews, in telling us about Esau, indicates that this was his bitter cry. Later, after having sold his birthright, when he would have inherited the blessing, he found no place for repentance. This does not mean that repentance was impossible; that God could not forgive. It simply means that try however hard he might, there was no way of going back and undoing the past. This same realization caused Omar Khayyam to exclaim: "The moving finger writes, and having writ moves on." Who is there among us who has not at one time or another faced this realization? The last member of my family to die was my youngest brother. I shall never forget how overwhelming was the realization that unkind actions and words, unconfessed, must forever stand in that way as far as he was concerned. There was simply nothing that I could do by way of going back and changing the past. When a bridge has been crossed, it is crossed; when a life has been lived, it is gone—there is no remedy, no panacea, that will call back and change the past.

(3) Finally, David's grief is made more bitter because the loss experienced in Absalom's life was so needless. He possessed a nagging fear that he could not shake off. Perhaps he thought: "Had I only been a better father, had I only acted differently and cast the right influence before him, had I only given more time to

him—perhaps everything would be fine now." David knew that he failed Absalom, and this failure brought the crushing blow to his spirit when he received the news of Absalom's death.

III. CAUSES OF DAVID'S FAILURE

In looking for an explanation concerning the sins of Absalom, one must not overlook the reality of the son's own guilt. He was a free moral agent before God and made decisions for himself. The principle of individual responsibility is grounded in the Bible. However, having said that, let us look behind the scenes at his background and environment. To be sure, he was not born a traitor; he was born with the capacity for treachery, but also with the capacity for faithfulness and loyalty. A group of people stood one day around the cradle of John the Baptist and asked: "What manner of child shall this be?" Who can ever answer a question like that? One thing is certain, and that is that parents and home usually determine the answer. Children so often encounter frightful hurdles in the homes where they live, from parents with whom they live, and from the moral climates in the areas where they live. Circumstances have a way of piling up in the path of a young life, and the child can be caught in a web from its tenderest years. Shakespeare said: "The evil that men do lives after them." There is an ancient simile which reads: "The soul of my lord is bound in the bundle of life." In Jeremiah 31:29 the great prophet says: "The fathers have eaten a sour grape, and the children's teeth are set on edge." Nowhere in the Bible is the truth of this maxim seen to clearer advantage than in David's life.

(1) David's failure resulted from neglect of his son. He gave his boy none of himself. Instead, he shifted the responsibility to the shoulders of others. Modern fathers cannot be too harsh on David. We must remember that he was a busy man, and therefore had many cares; but we cannot shut our eyes to the pathos of it all. David never really got acquainted with Absalom, never gained his

confidence, never won his heart. The chances are that not one time in his life did his father take him fishing or hunting. As a child, Absalom probably never thought of going to him with a broken toy; and as he grew older, why go to him with a broken heart? Absalom had everything but the one thing that he needed most—the companionship of a father. By neglecting Absalom, David lost a treasure far more priceless than any crown endangered by his rebellion.

Dr. Clovis Chappell, in his book, *Chappell's Special Day Sermons,* gives the following poem by an unknown author concerning a boy's musing about his father:

> He's the best thing, daddy is,
> When he ain't got the rheumatiz,
> Gives me pennies and good advice,
> 'Bout keeping clean and being nice,
> Saying please, and don't deceive,
> Handkerchief, instead of sleeve.
> Seems just like 'at daddy knew,
> He was once a small boy, too.
> Second table for him, I spec,
> With nothing but the chicken neck.
> Anyhow he always says,
> Give the kid the best there is.
> And when Ma sends me off to bed,
> He always takes the light ahead.
> And holds my hand and talks maybe,
> About the things that used to be,
> When he and Uncle was little boys,
> And all about their games and toys,
> What am I gonner be, Gee whiz,
> I'm gonner be like daddy is.
> I'd rather be like him, 'ijing,
> Than president or anything.

> He's like Ma says angels is
> When he ain't got the rheumatiz.

How David would have loved having his boy say such a thing about him, but the trouble was David was too busy. A great Baptist leader was heard to make this statement to a group of students: "The great tragedy of my life, as I think back over my role as a father, is the fact that I never learned to play with my children." A man in Louisville, Kentucky, made this remark: "My father left me fifty thousand dollars, but no kind words. I spent the money in sin. How much better off I would have been if he had left me not a dollar, but had taken up some of his time with me, played with me, been a pal, and left me some good, sound counsel and advice."

Another area where David tragically neglected Absalom was in an utter lack of discipline. All of his children reveal an undisciplined childhood. They grew up in luxury and license. Absalom murdered his brother, tried to steal the hearts of the people, rebelled, committed adultery with his father's wives, and tried to kill his own father. The writer of the book of Proverbs says in 29:15, "The rod and reproof give wisdom: but a child left to himself bringeth his mother to shame." The Bible specifically condemns parents who fail to discipline their children. In 1 Samuel 3:13, God says concerning the sinning sons of Eli: "For I have told him that I will judge his house for ever for the iniquity which he knoweth; because his sons made themselves vile, and he restrained them not!" Godly discipline could have made the difference in Absalom's life. A little boy once wrote an essay on the subject: "Why I Like My Mother Better Than Any Other Woman." In it he said: "I like my mother because she stays on talking terms with God and spanking terms with me." Needless to say, he won the contest.

(2) David's failure resulted from his own wrong example and influence. One cannot escape the feeling that David's grief is the bitter fruit of his own sin. David spared the rod, weakly indulged

Absalom to his own hurt. These were bad enough, but he placed an unsurmountable barrier in his pathway through his own immorality, which loosened the bonds of family purity. David became a prodigal, which perhaps made him ashamed to punish his own children. He let Absalom flaunt, swagger, and live in luxury with no curb. When his oldest son wanted a woman, he took her ruthlessly, even if she were his own half sister. After all, had not his father set the example? David murdered Bathsheba's husband. Why should not Absalom murder his own brother to punish him for a similar crime! The chasm rapidly widened until it ended in the tragic scene recorded in our Scripture passage. In the death of Absalom, David's chickens came home to roost.

Rachel had a worldly ambition for Jacob, aided him in defrauding his brother, and thus laid up sorrow that followed her to death. She never saw his face again. The effect of this action on Esau never was lifted. From that time on, Rachel's life was draped with the sombre clouds of mourning. This theme parents do not like! In 1938, Sinclair Lewis wrote a novel entitled, *Prodigal Parents*. It never became very popular. Why? Parents enjoy a thrilling tale about a prodigal son or daughter, but these same parents draw a line against any volume that points to the cause in prodigal parents. J. Edgar Hoover has been very pointed in saying: "Every new case that comes to my desk adds to the overwhelming evidence that when youth commits crime, a greater crime has already been committed in the home. The first responsibility rests upon parents!" We hear much these days about juvenile delinquency. What do we expect? When we sow the wind, we can only reap the whirlwind.

In conclusion, there are two things that must stick in our minds. First, the other side of David's grief witnesses to us of a self-sacrificing energy of a father's love. The dead son's faults are forgiven and forgotten. After all, the prodigal is still a son. The father is willing to die for the disobedient child. Such purity and depth of affection lives in human hearts. This noble characteristic is true of most parents and serves as an inspiration in spite of faults.

The final thing that we must not overlook is that David basically was a good man. He repented his terrible sin and God forgave him. However, his salvation did not bring salvation to his wayward boy. David made an excursion into the far country, and Absalom followed him. David came back from the far country, but so far as Absalom was concerned, he came alone. So often children are sacrificed upon the altar of thoughtless and selfish indulgence on the part of parents. The cost of such living is too frightfully high. God says: "Bring up a child in the way he should go, and when he is old, he will not depart from it." A well-known minister went to conduct a funeral service for the daughter in the home of a successful businessman—but it was a thoroughly worldly and godless home. On one side of the coffin sat the father. On the other side, the only other person present besides the minister was the father's intimate friend. Suddenly the father broke into speech, talking to himself more than to any other: "There is nothing in these things. You and I have been living for a good time and success. We have got everything we could during the week. We have been good poker players on Saturday night. We have spent our Sundays in the automobile and in social pleasures. We have put the club and the bank first, and my son has disgraced me with his shameless marriage, and my daughter is dead. I tell you there is only one place in which to bring up a family, and that is a Christian church. There is only one way to use Sunday for children, and that is to take them to church. What with money and wine and poker and pleasure all day Sunday, and parties all Sunday night, my family has been ruined. People don't know what the result of this kind of living will be until the end comes. But I know."

The lessons to be learned from such an example are all too obvious. David's life was filled with both happiness and sorrow. The blame for much of his sorrow lay in his own tragic blunders and sins. The value in meditating upon such a life is to be found in the practical lessons to be learned. These lessons will help us in a turbulent world to avoid the same pitfalls and will enable us to live at peace with conscience and with our God who holds us responsible for every failure.

MONEY TALKS!

I wonder if you have ever adopted the interesting little exercise of carrying on a conversation with an inanimate object? Try it with an antique automobile, a family heirloom, a giant redwood tree, or an old building. Try it on the word, "money." Without a doubt, money is a charming word and is "as musical as dream-bells sounding on the sloping hills of sleep." One of the most familiar terms in our day is "money talks." And indeed it does. A common jingle runs: "If money talks, as some folks tell, to most of us it says, 'Farewell!' "

Money has a language all its own. Take a one-, five-, or ten-dollar bill in your hand and then let your imagination jump back across the years to the day that it came from the Bureau of Engraving. Trace it across the years until it returns to the Bureau for destruction. My, what a story it would relate—the places it has been, the things it has been used for, the types of people who have had it, the harm it has done, the good that it might have accomplished, etc. Think of what it would say if it could tell its own story. There is a great deal more than mere poetry in this little poem:

A big silver dollar and a little brown cent
Rolling along together went,
Rolling along on the smooth sidewalk,
"You poor little cent, you cheap little mite,
I am bigger and twice as bright.

I am worth more than you a hundred-fold
And written on me in letters bold
Is the motto drawn from a pious creed;
'In God We Trust,' which all may read."
"Yes, I know all that," said the little brown cent.
'Tis true I'm just a cheap little mite.
And I know I'm not big, nor pretty, nor bright;
And yet,' said the little cent with a meek little sigh,
'You don't go to church as often as I.' "

The life of King David and his relationship to his son Absalom provide a perfect illustration of the inability of money and material things really to produce happiness and personal success. Listen to the different types of speeches money might make:

(1) It may say, "Clutch me and hoard me and I will dry the fountains of sympathy and benevolence in your soul, and leave you barren and destitute. Grasp me tightly and I will change your eyes that they will care to look upon nothing that does not contain my image, and so transform your ears that my soft, metallic ring or subtle rustle will sound louder than the cries of needy people and wail of the perishing multitudes. Store me away, clutch me, and I will destroy your sympathy for the human race, your respect for the right, and your love and reverence for Almighty God."

(2) On the other hand it may say, "Spend me for self and not for others and I will harden your heart and make you indifferent to everything except your own pleasures and desires."

I AM MONEY

Dug from the mountainside, washed in the glen,
Servant am I, or the master of men;
   Steal me, I curse you,
   Earn me, I bless you,
Grasp me and hoard me, a fiend shall possess you.
   Lie for me, die for me,

Covet me, take me,
Angel or devil, I am what you make me.
MONEY.

(3) Or money may say, "Give me away for the benefit of others and I will return in streams of spiritual revenue to your soul. I cannot buy you personal happiness, health, or heaven. I can aid in bringing health and joy to you when I am rightly used. I can care for orphans, heal the sick, provide Christian education, look after the aged and unfortunate, send missionaries to the whole world, build churches and carry on ministries and spread peace and goodwill to others. I will bless the one that receives me and the one that gives me. I will supply food and raiment and relief for suffering, while at the same time I will secure joy and peace for the soul that uses me rightly."

7.

The Christian View of Death and Life

(Luke 24:1–9; 2 Timothy 1:7–13)

The apostle Paul says in 2 Timothy 1:10, "Christ . . . hath abolished death, and hath brought life and immorality to light through the gospel." This is indeed the day death died.

Many centuries ago there was an epoch-making book of theological thought written by Anselm, entitled, *Why Did God Become a Man?* There are many answers to that question as well as various interpretations, but you will not find a better answer than the one given in the Word of God. In the book of Hebrews, the writer speaks of the birth of Jesus Christ in this way: "Forasmuch then as the children are partakers of flesh and blood, he also himself likewise took part of the same; that through death he might destroy him that hath the power of death, that is, the devil; and deliver them who through fear of death were all their lifetime subject to bondage. For verily he took not on him the nature of angels; but he took on him the seed of Abraham." This deliverance was effected by the dying of the Lord Jesus Christ! His death upon the cross was no accident! It was not the result of the high priest being too clever or too powerful for him; but, was of his own design and purpose, voluntary and self-chosen. He died! He died in order to win deliverance for all mankind. *Only by dying could he nullify the power of Satan over human life and the fear of death.*

There are many things Christ did for our race. We could spend a long time talking about all the wonderful blessings that accrue to us because Jesus Christ came into the world and lived, taught, died, and came forth from the grave. But I am concerned about only one here and it is the thing that Paul mentions in 2 Timothy 1:10, his deliverance from the enslaving fear of death!

I readily admit that this subject can be overdone, that it indeed is morbid for a person to think and to talk too much about death. But at the same time, it is foolish and disastrous not to think about it and not to talk about it at all. We must face realities! This is not something that will go away if we turn our backs and refuse to admit that it is a reality; we cannot play ostrich and hide our heads in the sands of wishful thinking and say to death, "Now, be gone!" Death is very real!

In 2 Timothy 1:10 Paul mentions three words which are the three most tremendous words in the English language, and also the three things upon which men most earnestly and diligently seek for light: death, life, and immortality or resurrection. These are the things about which we are most concerned. God's Word garrisons our hearts against the hour when death comes, bringing healing for stricken and bleeding hearts in all of life's experiences.

I. THE FACT OF DEATH

There are very crucial, critical questions about death. Before we can answer them, though, we must face the reality of death. We must admit there is such a thing as death.

A prominent businessman lay on his deathbed. He called his closest friend to the bedside and instructed him about what to do with his remains. "Take the mortal remains and cremate them." The friend asked, "What shall I do with the ashes." He said, "Do with them? Just mail them to the Department of Internal Revenue and tell them that now they have everything!" Death and taxes are inevitable!

Mark Twain once said, "This life is a losing proposition; nobody gets out of it alive." The ancient Jews had an old saying that went like this: "In this life, death never suffers a man to be glad or joyous." The Greeks and Romans could teach us much about death, especially concerning the brevity of life and the certainty of death. They would come together for their great feasts and banquets. At either end of the banqueting table they would place a skeleton as a silent reminder that although they were then eating, drinking, and making merry, very soon they must leave this world and everything in it. This is the bitterness in every cup that we must drink. This is the discord in every bit of music on earth. Indeed, this is the dread that haunts men day and night. Death is a reality!

Do you realize that every second that ticks by on the clock, somewhere in the world some person dies? Do you realize that out of the total population of the earth every year we have 40 million deaths? You cannot pick up the paper and look through it without seeing obituary columns and reading about tragic deaths.

What does the Bible have to say about death? The Bible says to us that we human beings are immortal, undying spirits living in a house of clay which is flimsy, subject to disease, flesh, bone, and blood. The Bible speaks of our bodies as being temples; therefore, we are *temple dwellers*. When death comes, there is a separation of the spirit from the body. When the hour comes that the body no longer is inhabitable because of old age, disease, or something else, the Bible speaks of the spirit as moving out of the house of clay, the tenement in which we dwell. The Bible says that "it is appointed unto men once to die." The Bible says that for everything there is a season: there is a time to plant, there is a time to pluck up; a time to sow and a time to reap; a time to live and a time to die. We cannot get away from it; it is a fact, and nobody escapes it. Let us face squarely the fact of death.

II. THE FEAR OF DEATH

Next, we must face this harrowing fear that we have for death. There are many things that enslave us, but there is no enslavement quite equal to the enslavement of fear, no matter what kind of fear it might be. Think of the person who has commited a crime, who has the fear of a guilty conscience. From that moment on he begins to dodge people. It seems that everybody pursues him; always the long hand of the law reaches out to clutch him; he is uncomfortable night and day because his conscience disturbs him and he continues to flee. For him it is a very disturbing experience. But, there is no enslavement to fear quite equal to the fear of death, as God says here in his word.

What is the cure for our fear of death? Turn the light on! *We will never be able to live victoriously until we are convinced that there is nothing in death for us to fear.* Theodore Roosevelt, when Quentin Roosevelt lost his life in war, made this remark: "Only those are fit to live who are not afraid to die."

Why is it that men fear death? The Bible indicates that there are several reasons. One of them is our fear of losing that which we have accumulated. Our fear of being separated from this mundane world in which we live, the materials which we accumulate— houses and lands, real estate, stocks, bonds, gold, silver, estates, pictures, medals that we have won, things that are very dear to our hearts. We cannot bear the thought of separation from these material things; thus we fear death for that reason.

We fear death because of the physical pain involved in it. But let me hasten to say that not always does death involve physical pain. How often people slip out to meet the Lord while they are asleep, and there is no physical pain involved at all. We often pray that we might be spared the experience of pain at the last moment. But at the same time, we know that in too many cases pain is involved. There is enough pain involved to make us all apprehensive of the end, and thus we fear death.

We are afraid of being torn loose from our moorings and plunged out into the unknown—a world that we know nothing about as far as our experience is concerned. Who has not read Hamlet's soliloquy and marveled at the insight that William Shakespeare possessed?

He was reasoning thus;

To die, to sleep,
To sleep; perchance to dream; ay, there's the rub;
For in that sleep of death what dreams may come
When we have shuffled off this mortal coil,
Must give us pause. There's the respect
That makes calamity of so long life;
For who would bear the ships and scorns of time,
The oppressor's wrong, the proud man's contumely,
The pangs of despis'd love, the law's delay,
The insolence of office, and the spurns
That patient merit of the unworthy takes,
When he himself might his quietus make
With a bare bodkin? Who would fardels bear,
To grunt and sweat under a weary life,
But that the dread of something after death,
The undiscover'd country from whose bourne
No traveller returns, puzzles the will
And makes us rather bear those ills we have
Than fly to others that we know not of?

To be cut loose from a real world, and plunged out into the unknown world—this is our fear, and it is like a child's fear of the darkness.

However, I am persuaded that our greatest fear is not at the point of our fear of physical pain or material separation. *Our greatest fear is at the point of our sense of sin and our fear of divine judgment that follows death.* After all, that is what God warns about in his Word. "The sting of death is sin, and the strength of sin is the law." "It is appointed unto men once to die, but after that the judgment." And so, with an overwhelming sense of guilt upon us, we hesitate to be plunged out into the unknown to meet God at the judgment bar. I could be completely wrong, but, in my opinion, death in our world was not God's original intention for his children, because *sin and death* are too closely associated in the Word of God. Ezekiel, the prophet, tells us about man's spiritual death in these words, "It is not my will that any should perish." That is the voice of God. I also believe that originally it was not God's intention that man even die physically. Have you ever thought what would happen had man never departed from obedience to God, had man never rebelled against him, had sin never become a reality in our world? I think we have a glimpse of it in what happened to Enoch when he walked with God. The writer of the book of Genesis says, "Enoch walked with God and was not, for God took him." The writer of the book of Hebrews says about him: "By faith, Enoch was translated that he should not see death and was not found because God translated him. For before his translation he had this testimony, that he pleased God."

III. HOW CHRIST ABOLISHED DEATH

Paul says, and the entire Bible proclaims, that Jesus Christ, in the glorious resurrection of his body from the grave, hath "abolished death!" Right here we are not concerned with the many "infallible proofs" of his resurrection that the Bible tells us about. They are there, and I trust that every reader believes what God says in his Word about the resurrection of Christ. That is not the burden of this message. The burden of our message is the primary meaning of the word "abolished," in connection with the death and the resurrection of Jesus Christ. "Abolish" means to make of no effect, to void, to make empty. This means then that his resurrection emptied death of everything that death held in the way of fear as far as men are concerned. It does not mean that he has taken away the dissolution of the body. That is not what is involved at all. But, even this has ceased to be the ugly, hideous thing that men have in mind when they talk about death. What he does mean is that Christ defeated death, that it would no longer be the frightful contradiction and dissipation of all the hopes of human hearts. The eyes of the disciples beheld the Master dying upon the cross, watched him slip out into eternity, waited through those agonizing hours and days, until Easter morning; and then they watched him come back to tell them about what was on the other side. That's the important thing! The poet has said this: "Flood has lost its chill since Jesus crossed the river."

What was left for these disciples to be afraid of? If at one point in history the death tyrant's grip had been broken, then his reign was then destroyed. I like these words of Karl Heim's: "Just as when a dyke in the Low Countries on the shores of the North Sea gives way, even if it is only one little section, we know that, although this is in itself an event of small importance, the consequences are incalculable: Beyond the dyke is the tumultuous sea, which will burst through the opening—so Paul knew when he had met the Risen One, that 'He is the first-born of them that slept!' " [1] And the dyke has broken. Now light is here, and the blinding power of the devil has once and for all been dissipated. This is the meaning of the word, 'abolished.' According to John on Patmos, Jesus said to him: "I am the First and the Last, the Alpha and the Omega. I am he that liveth and was dead, and behold, I am alive forevermore."

Now, turn the light on. Look at these fears that we have been discussing. Nothing is quite so good in the dark as truth and light. What were those fears?

First of all, the fear of losing that which we have accumulated. How often Jesus endeavored to get us to see that things do not last, and that we ought not to build our hearts, lives, hopes, dreams, and aspirations upon material things that change and pass away. He urged that we shun things that moth and rust corrupt and thieves can steal. "What doth it profit a man to gain the whole world and lose his own soul?" He said that not only can we not take it with us, but he tried to get us to see that in most cases we cannot even keep it while we are here on this earth. Talk about leaving material things, separated from them, Jesus battled that philosophy all through his ministry.

Then, there is fear of physical pain. There are two things I want
to say about this fear. First, you and I ought not to anticipate
trouble that has not come. The manner of our going when the end
comes is entirely in the hands of a loving Father and not at our
discretion. Second, Christ will be with us by his promise to give
us the grace that we need in the hour in which we need it most.
Oh, how many verses, how many times, the Bible proclaims this
marvelous truth. "We know that all things work together for good
to those who love the Lord, who are called according to his purposes." "He will not suffer you to be tempted above that ye are
able to bear it." "Lo, I am with you always, even unto the end."
"Call upon me in the day of trouble, and I will deliver thee and
thou shalt glorify me." "I will neither leave thee nor forsake thee."
"Yea, though I walk through the valley of the shadow of death,
I will fear no evil, for thou art with me." What joy and strength
are ours!

Another very real fear is the fear of disembodiment, of being
plunged out into the unknown. My friend, Jesus came back pur-
posely in order to tell us what is on the other side. The child of
God needs not fear what God has in store for him. How often in
the Bible we are told that there is another side, there is another
world. Jesus said, "In my Father's house are many mansions." He
tells us that his Father's home is more beautiful, it is fairer, it is
far happier than anything that we know here on this earth. All of
this God has provided for those who love him. "Eye hath not seen,
nor ear heard, and neither hath entered into the heart of man the
things which God hath provided for those who love him." "If the
earthly house of this tabernacle were dissolved, we have a building
from God, a house not made with hands, eternal in the heavens."
Thus the Scriptures would counteract the fear of the unknown and
what it holds for us.

The final and greatest of all fears is the fear of the burden of sin
and of the judgment of God hereafter. Here, as is true in all fear,
there is no solution other than faith. Faith alone has the answer.

What a wonderful gospel we proclaim! What a glorious gospel this Book presents to us! In Isaiah 53 I find these words: "He is despised and rejected of men; a man of sorrows, and acquainted with grief: and we hid as it were our faces from him; he was despised, and we esteemed him not. Surely he hath borne our griefs, and carried our sorrows: yet we did esteem him stricken, smitten of God, and afflicted. But he was wounded for our transgressions; he was bruised for our iniquities: the chastisement of our peace was upon him; and with his stripes we are healed." Also, Peter, in 1 Peter 2:24, said: "Who his own self bare our sins in his own body on the tree."

What is the answer to human sin and to divine judgment in the hereafter? There is no answer, no solution, apart from Jesus Christ, "who hath abolished death and brought life and immortality to light through the gospel.

IV. THE CHRISTIAN CONCEPT OF DEATH

Jesus Christ has paved the way for a new concept of death. What is the proper Christian attitude? *Death is merely a portal* that admits us out into eternity and into the joys of God. There is no cessation of being; there is no eclipse of consciousness. The Bible tells us that we go right on living—and, mind you, living with the Lord—which is the important thing.

We greatly need this message in our day with the ravages of disease laying waste human life and with the threat of mass destruction under which we must live constantly. Actually, the trumpets of God ought to blast a victorious note every time we lay aside the mortal remains of a loved one who died believing in Jesus Christ. It is a day of victory for that person! I have a book, which I treasure very highly, written by Catherine Marshall, entitled, *A Man Called Peter.* It is a biography of Peter Marshall, her husband, a great saint of God, who was pastor of the New York Avenue Presbyterian Church in Washington, D.C., and also Chaplain of the Senate. The last chapter deals with his fatal illness. Catherine Marshall tells about how the ambulance came for him during the night, and when the attendants carried him out of the house on a stretcher, he looked up into her face at the door, and said to her, "Darling, I will see you in the morning." Well, I am sure that he was thinking about seeing her the next day when she came to visit him at the hospital. He probably did not realize the attack would prove fatal. Catherine Marshall, looking back upon the experience, and those words, said the experience had become most meaningful.[2] His last words form the victorious shout of every child of God. Did not Jesus Christ in the upper room say to his disciples, "I will see you again"? Did he not come forth from the grave and by his resurrection give us assurance that we too would come forth from the grave? Therefore, to the child of God who buries the remains of a loved one, this ought to be his shout too: "Darling, I'll see you in the morning." This is the most important matter with which we mortals have to deal. "Absent from the body, present with the Lord."

The year was 1666 when Hugh Mackail, youngest and bravest of the Covenanting preachers, was brought before his judges and condemned to the scaffold. They gave him four days to live: then back to Tolbooth the soldiers led him. Many in the watching crowd wept as he went—so young he seemed, so terrible his coming fate. But in his own eyes no tears were seen, no trace of self-pity or regret on the radiant, eager face of this young Galahad of the cross. "Trust in God!" he cried, and his eyes were shining—"Trust in God!" Then, suddenly catching a glimpse of a friend among the crowd, "Good news," he cried, "good news! I am within four days' journey of enjoying the sight of Jesus Christ!"[3] "Absent from the body; present with the Lord!" God gave us another significant word to use and we ought to use it much more than we do. In speaking of death, we ought to use the word that Jesus Christ gives us, and it is the word "sleep," instead of death. He gave us this word because of what it means and implies. "Our friend, Lazarus, sleepeth," he said. Stephen "fell on sleep." Paul said, "Even so them also which sleep in Jesus will God bring with him." He has emancipated us from the fear of death, and therefore you and I can shout as Paul shouted, "O death, where is thy sting? O grave, where is thy victory?" He has liberated us from the dread of corruption.

The most comforting thing on earth to the Christian's heart is to know that he never goes through an experience except that God's power and presence are right with him. This is especially meaningful as he contemplates death.

> When I come to the river at ending of day,
>   When the last winds of sorrow have blown;
> There'll be somebody waiting to show me the way,
>   I won't have to cross Jordan alone.
> Oftentimes I'm forsaken, and weary, and sad,
>   When it seems that my friends have all gone;
> There is one tho't that cheers me and makes my heart
>   glad,
>   I won't have to cross Jordan alone.
> Tho' the billows of sorrow and trouble may sweep,
>   Christ the Saviour will care for his own;
> Till the end of the journey, my soul he will keep,
>   I won't have to cross Jordan alone.
> I won't have to cross Jordan alone.
>   Jesus died for my sins to atone;
> When the darkness I see,
>   He'll be waiting for me,
> I won't have to cross Jordan alone.[4]

Dr. Alexander Maclaren was one of the greatest preachers this world has ever known. He tells about an experience that he had when he was a boy, just a mere wisp of a lad. He had left home for the first time. He said that his daddy had secured him a job six miles from his home in Glasgow. On Monday morning his father walked the distance with him to his new work. When he left him there, he gave him specific instructions to come home Saturday night after work. Alexander Maclaren said that between his job and his home in Glasgow there was a deep, dark ravine that was dreaded and shunned by people everywhere in the countryside because known criminals and wild beasts inhabited the area. It was a desolate place, and yet his daddy had given him instructions; therefore, he must go home alone on Saturday night. He lived in terror the whole week—day and night he thought about that trip. When he finished on Saturday evening, he got his few belongings together and started out into the night as his daddy had told him to do. He came to the mouth of the ravine and stopped there in the darkness, crouching against the wall behind a bush, because in the darkness he heard footsteps coming up out of the ravine. He said that his heart pounded within him as though it would jump completely out of his mouth. He was stricken with terror and horror. Then he detected a rhythm to those footsteps that he recognized. Suddenly he saw a head and shoulders coming up out of the darkness that were most familiar to him. His daddy had come to walk through the ravine with him. He placed his hand in the hand of his daddy's, and as he went down into that ravine he was afraid of nothing in the world. His daddy was the greatest man on earth, and with him by his side, there was nothing to fear. Oh, my friend, that is exactly what Jesus Christ promises to do for each one of us. "He hath abolished death and brought life and immortality to light through the gospel."

With a firm faith in God and his promises, we can live victoriously as we walk just one step at a time.

LIVING LIFE A DAY AT A TIME

"Take therefore no thought for the morrow: for the morrow shall take thought for the things of itself. Sufficient unto the day is the evil thereof" (Matt. 6:32).

In a very popular television entitled, "Run for Your Life," each episode took as its starting point information supplied to Hero by his doctor that he had only a limited time to live. His adventures were designed to enable him to see and enjoy life because he had only today for which to live.

An anxious patient, lying on her sickbed, turned to her doctor and asked: "Doctor, how long shall I have to lie here and suffer?" The wise and kind physician answered: "Just a day at a time!" As we turn the crisp new pages of our calendars, let us determine that into each bright numeral we will, God willing, pour twenty-four hours of real living. God has never promised to any human being the fact that he will still be alive in the flesh tomorrow. He gives us today and the day comes to us with its burdens, its duties, its hopes, and its fears. Thank God we do not have to live a week at a time and make all of the decisions involved in that week, but only one day at a time. Tomorrow is never ours until it becomes today. It is a blessed secret, this living just a day at a time. Any person who has seen the crushing burden of his sin lifted by Calvary's Cross can carry his own little burden, however heavy, until night-fall. Any person who knows that his Saviour has completed the tremendous work of his redemption can do his own work, however hard, just for one day. Any person who has beheld the patience of his Lord can live patiently, lovingly, helpfully—until the sun goes down. Then God gives us the nighttime to shut down the curtain of darkness on our little days. We cannot see beyond, nor do we need to. Tomorrow is in his hands. He asks us only to live today.

A person who looks at the responsibilities of a whole year or even a month might be overwhelmed. But, let us remember that God has cut the year and the month into smaller pieces and commanded that we live "just a day at a time."

In Deuteronomy 33, he has promised us that as our days, so shall our strength ever be. We have his assurance that each day will find us equipped with that amount of strength that will be necessary to bear its burden, to endure its trial, and to fight its battle through.

---

[1] James S. Stewart, *A Faith to Proclaim* (New York: Scribner's, 1953), p. 134.

[2] Robert E. Luccock, *If God Be for Us* (New York: Harper, 1954), p. 182.

[3] Stewart, James S., *The Strong Name* (New York: Scribner's, 1941), p. 249.

[4] Copyright 1934. Renewal 1962. Broadman Press. All rights reserved. Used by permission.

8.

High Level Life in a Space Age

(Isaiah 40:31)

It has only been a matter of some three short decades since the atomic bomb was dropped on Hiroshima and Nagasaki, blasting these cities into limbo and marking the end of one age and the beginning of an entirely new one for man on this planet. Since that date, things have happened with such amazing rapidity that we have seen the imaginary world of Jules Verne become a reality before our eyes. Some wag has said, "The atomic age is here to stay, but are we?"

Indeed, we live in a changing world. It always has been such. Dr. E. Stanley Jones said, "There is nothing new in saying that we live in an age of transition." Someone has facetiously remarked that when Adam and Eve were going out of the Garden of Eden, Adam turned to Eve and said, "My dear, this is an age of transition." The oldest known bit of writing in the world is a piece of papyrus in a Constantinople museum. On it is written: "Alas, times are not what they used to be. Children no longer obey their parents, and everyone wants to write a book." Another has said, "The only permanent thing is change."

Once men thought that the earth was the center of the universe and the sky spread over it like a huge inverted bowl, but along came Copernicus and Galileo with their telescopes, observations, and calculations. They revealed to the world the startling fact that the earth is only a tiny speck revolving about the sun which actually is the center of the universe. And so, the old order changed! It was once believed that the earth was flat, but along came Christopher Columbus to sail to its rim and beyond its rim, and thus discover that the earth actually is round. And so, the old order changeth! Men once believed in the divine right of kings. Then something happened in the name of democracy, liberty, fraternity, and equality. The old order changed! One of the great turning points in the history of mankind was the Industrial Revolution: steamboat, cotton gin, telephone, electric lights, machinery, automobile, radio, airplane, and the old order changed. War once had a romantic appeal. It was limited to soldiers on the battlefield. Now the real sufferers are defenseless cities, women, children, the aged and the helpless—and so the old order changed.

In this age of nuclear power, ICBM's, guided missiles, devastating rockets, astronauts, and earth satellites, we all recognize clearly enough that we live in a space age. Scientific genius continues to amaze us with repeated space achievements.

Reactions to space achievements are quite varied: From a political and military point of view, many see them as a gigantic step forward in scientific progress, a wild scramble for control of the universe. Some view the events skeptically and have yet to be convinced that a landing on the moon really was made. Some are fearful that contacts with celestial bodies may lead to a chain reaction and the utter destruction of the universe. Some are bewildered and puzzled by these developments, and ask what it all means and where we are headed.

In the face of scientific progress, there is one tremendous truth which emerges: Man must not permit his inventive genius to outstrip his moral character and spiritual development. Somewhere along the way there must be a shift in emphasis. "Misguided men" must rise to know how to control "guided missiles." Man by his nature and equipment was ordained of God from the beginning of time to be the lord and master of the earth on which he lives. Made in the image of God, equipped with a brain and a personality, man has the ability to live on this earth like a man, as well as to soar in space like an astronaut. A lad with an observing eye, after staring in wonderment at the towering trunks of the giant redwoods in California, turned to his father and said: "It's funny, isn't it, Dad? You never see any of these big trees down in the valley. I guess they were made for higher altitudes." Man was also made for high altitudes.

He was designed for greatness. The highest compliment that can be paid to any creature is, "It is almost human." Yet, the word "human" has come to be used as a synonym for the low and lewd. In an effort to gloss over and excuse human frailties, people often will remark, "Well, after all, he is only human, you know!" Man's God-given capacities and nature fit him for living at high altitudes—for nobility, heroism, honor, righteousness, idealism, self-sacrifice, holy adventure. When Jesus stopped the funeral procession on the outskirts of the village of Nain, he actually spoke to the whole human race when he said, "Young man, I say unto thee, Arise!"

I. DIFFERENT LEVELS IN LIFE

Our Declaration of Independence says: "We hold these truths to be self-evident, that all men are created equal, that they are endowed by their Creator with certain unalienable Rights, that among these are Life, Liberty, and the pursuit of Happiness." The statement is both true and untrue. It is true that all men are created equal spiritually, being potentially the sons of God, and of each and every one being of equal importance in God's eyes. But it is untrue from the angle of native endowment, human will and determination, and the material circumstances in which we are born and live. The Master of men came to bring the abundant life, and desired that all people aspire to live upon the higher levels in every area of life. To master and to survive in our space age, life must be full and complete. It is not full unless the different levels are recognized and the needs thereof satisfied.

(1) *Physical.* Too many people remain satisfied with a bare margin of good health, and of life's goods. Like the hermit who exists

in his dark, dank cave when the fresh, bright world waits just outside; like a sick creature who clings in a tiny cage when the door is open to the joys of liberty. Many people never rise above the material. There is a story concerning a Scotsman who took a boat trip once and lived on cheese and crackers. At the end of his journey, he learned that his ticket had called for three square meals per day at no extra charge.

The Bible declares that these bodies of ours are holy, being the temples of God's Spirit. Anything that mistreats and hurts the physical body is a sin against human nature and against the God who gave us life. A young man once found a five dollar bill on the street. After that time he never looked up when he walked. During a lifetime he accumulated 29,519 buttons, 54,172 pins, 22 cents, a bent back and a miserable disposition. How many of us there are who miss some wonderful things in life by looking only at the material!

(2) *Intellectual.* Well do we know that there are many different levels of intellectual attainment. Different people are content with various degrees of education. Some deny themselves the friendliness of good books. To miss these and fail to develop one's intellectual capacities to the highest extent is to miss the joy of accomplishment, and to exist on cheese and crackers in a world of educational opportunities.

(3) *Aesthetic and Cultural.* Music, poetry, and art present levels of life which dawdlers in the valley never enjoy.

(4) *Vocational.* What are your future plans? Which level have you chosen for yourself? Are you aiming for the top, or just interested in getting by? Is your purpose in this world to get rich or to invest your life? It is at this point that great souls rise to sublime heights and selfish people live a miserable shrinking existence.

(5) *Moral and Spiritual.* In an age of scientific advance, we have experienced a moral and spiritual lag in our country. Our young people need to face frankly the great need of purposeful living,

instead of sinking to the level of spineless, jellyfish, everybody-does-it existence. In our world of confusion and darkness, we need to stand up and be counted, like the old man I read about recently. Every Sunday he would take his Bible under his arm and walk through the small town where he lived to Sunday School and church. For the last five years of his life he was deaf. He never understood a word of the Sunday School lesson or of the sermon by his pastor—yet he continued to go. One day his son-in-law asked, "Grandpa, why do you keep on going to Sunday School and church when you cannot hear a word that is said?" He replied, "What would my neighbors think if they saw me sitting on the porch rocking while Sunday School and church were going on? I keep on going even though I cannot hear because I want people to know whose side I am on."

II. REACHING THE HIGHEST LEVEL

Before one can climb he must be ready and willing to pay the price. Our government is going to enormous expenses and using every conceivable test to thoroughly train and equip astronauts for flight into outer space. In order to climb and to live life at the highest level, these things are absolutely essential:

(1) *Proper equipment.* This is almost trite and, yet it is basic. Whether a person is going to skin-dive, climb a mountain, or take a flight into outer space, one of his first considerations is that of good equipment. For the highest and noblest living you must be equipped with: convictions, vision, determination, enthusiasm, courage, and a profound faith in God and in humanity.

(2) *Willingness to accept the advice of experts.* To make a success in life, seek advice and truth from proper and reliable sources. Teachers and parents are so often considered "behind the times" by youth. They forget that age, maturity, and experience are great teachers within themselves. It was a very wise commencement speaker who reasoned thus with a graduating class: "I commend

you for your wonderful attainments. You have indeed come a long way in your development. You have learned much." With this reasoning they nodded agreement. Then he added, "Even though you are graduating, you do not intend to cease learning, and go through life with an arrested intellectual development, do you?" They even agreed with this. Then he said, "Go home then, and listen to your parents, they have about twenty-five years start on you!"

Bishop Arthur Moore several years ago offered a timely warning at this point: "You can go down to the newsstand in almost any city and buy magazines containing articles on how to live written by authors who have never themselves risen above the gutter." Jesus of Nazareth, the Founder and the Head of the Christian religion, was a Master in the matter of living life to its fullest. Familiarize yourself with his life and the great principles which he taught.

(3) *Purposeful living.* Before you can expect to accomplish anything in life, you must set some worthy goals or objectives for yourself. The apostle Paul said, "This one thing I do." An unknown poet has put it in these words:

> The heights by great men reached and kept,
>   Were not attained by sudden flight;
> But they, while their companions slept,
>   Were toiling upward in the night.

The trouble with too many of us is that we are not going any place. We resemble the old bear in the bit of doggerel that says:

> There was an old bear in the zoo
> Who was feeling exceedingly blue.
> "It bores me, you know, to walk to and fro,
> I'll reverse it, I'll walk fro and to."

Samuel Wilberforce, in a letter to Gladstone, advised: "Act now with a view to then." Thomas Edison kept a book two inches thick, full of figures and drawings, which he said contained one hundred years of work. He had outlined his life's activities for one hundred years—things that should be done and things that would be done; and he said he had made arrangements for all these things to be completed after he was dead. Now, that is projecting one's life into the future, isn't it? A young woman looking at Raphael's painting of the School of Athens, in the University of Virginia, said to Noah K. Davis that Alexander of Macedon in the picture did not look like a conqueror; he was too dreamy. Noah Davis replied, "He who would conquer the world must first dream that he has conquered it."

III. DISTINGUISHING MARKS OF HIGH LEVEL LIFE

In mountain climbing, when you get up above timber line, you will find the finest game, the most beautiful flowers, the freshest air, the longest view, and the clearest vision. The same applies when a person leaves the valleys and gutters of life and seeks diligently to rise and live on the high level. Three things will characterize such living:

(1) Main interest in life and not in things.

(2) Majors on others and not on self.

(3) More concern about the eternal instead of the temporal.

The master secret of attaining and living the abundant life is to keep one's eyes on the every-youthful Christ. He is ever young, zestful, and challenging. Our childhood concept of God as being a grandfatherly old man is all wrong. The God of the Bible is young, buoyant, enthusiastic—a God of creative energy, rolling stars up the skies and flinging planets from his fingertips. He is the God of new life, the springtime and the dawn. It is we who grow old, simply because we do not maintain fellowship with him. Let us heed the admonition of our text: "They that wait upon the Lord, shall renew their strength . . . !"

Such people reveal that they have hidden springs of strength and endurance.

ENDURANCE

Cyrus Albertson was a maker of violins. He made his living by another vocation, but he found expression for his genius by making violins. He not only made them, but played them so well that few men in all the mountain country could release such singing music. He told this story a few years ago in *The Christian Advocate*. Someone asked him one day, "Where do you get the wood you use in the violins?" He answered, "At first, I went to the wood yards and looked for logs of hard wood, wood from the southlands and from over the many seas. Always, when a violin was finished, some quality of tone had eluded me. Now, I have found it. This one is made from wood at timberline. Timberline! The last stand of trees—twelve thousand feet into the heavens, where trees take on strange shapes, where timberline gives them personality. This one is of timberline spruce. It has resonance."

Think on that for a moment and let your nerves tingle with the thrill of it. Resonance from timberline! If you have ever been above timberline and felt the sharp wind that blows, then you can fully appreciate the remark. If you have ever seen the storms blown from the clouds, branches of trees tossed about like feathers, trees bent to their knees, their branches down asunder with ice and sleet, then you will understand. The timberline trees are the heroes of the high country. Easy living did not put resonance into the wood that became the perfect violin. Simple logic dictates that easy living never puts resonance into our lives. An unknown author has penned the following little verse:

> You will find that luck
> Is only pluck
> To try things over and over;
> Patience and skill,
> Courage and will,
> Are the four leaves of luck's clover.

All of us have read the story of the little plucky frog. There were two, you recall, that hopped gaily into the springhouse. Great crocks of milk were placed on low shelves over the cool, bubbling water. Curiosity led the frogs to hop up on the edge of a deep crock of cream, soon to be made into butter. Losing their balance, they both fell into the cream with a splash. One frog came to the top, swam to the edge of the crock, and finding it was too slippery to climb, sank to the bottom and promptly went to Frog Land. The other, when he came to the surface, swam round and round, kicking vigorously for hours and hours. He simply refused to give up. Strange to relate, when the housewife came to the springhouse for the cream, she found a small pat of butter in the crock, while perched up on top of it was an exhausted frog. But, he was alive!

9.

The Truth About Hate

(1 John 2:3–11; 3:15)

In the coach of a train sat a sophisticated young woman, highly cultured, dressed in the height of fashion, but one whose spirits visibly drooped. Seated next to her was a minister by the name of Lance Webb. She was not aware that he was a minister, however, and she began to toss off bits of her philosophy. It was evident that she had suffered very greatly—two divorces and a third marriage now going to pieces.

"Love? What is love?" she asked. And, without waiting for an answer, she gave her own definition: "Love is a sickly sentiment that puts a romantic wrapping on a shoddy counterfeit. It remains only for a few days until it is discovered to be a sham. If only . . ." and her voice trailed off then for a moment of complete silence. Then, she continued speaking slowly and broodingly: "If only someone would invent or discover a pill that people could take night and morning that would take out all the nasty temper, the venom of envy and green-eyed jealousy, the harsh unkindness, the stinking selfishness and resentement—well, then their love could be real and beautiful, and life would be worth living!"

Then she added, almost viciously, as she turned toward the preacher, "Why hasn't someone done that before now? They have discovered medicine that takes out the fever and kills the germs of disease. Why hasn't somebody discovered something that will make *real love* possible?"

Indeed, they have. Paul gives the prescription over here in the book of Galatians: "Now the fruit of the spirit is love, joy, peace, patience, kindness . . . gentleness [good temper]." In other words, in the Divine relationship, there is available to every person, through Jesus Christ, something that does make love real and make it possible.

John, in these verses from his first epistle, sees personal relationships in terms of black and white. There are no halfway stages, John says. Dr. Westcott, commenting upon these verses, said: "Indifference is impossible. There is no twilight in the spiritual world." And he is speaking of man's attitude toward his fellowman, right where we live. The man next door, the man with whom we live or work, the person with whom we have contact regularly. He is talking to the man who preaches love for the heathen, but will put forth no effort in terms of fellowship with the person next door. He is talking about the person who talks about love for other nations and other individuals, but right within his own home or family circle is not able to live in peace.

Now, I think he is perfectly right in drawing a thin, sharp line right down the middle, and showing that there is a distinction here between light and darkness, between love and hate. My friend, we cannot escape other people. No matter how hard we try, we cannot escape them.

Let me ask you a question: How do you regard your fellowman? Dr. William Barclay answers that question in five ways. He says that there are five responses people make to others:

1. The love response. That is that every other man is my fellow human being. He is my earthly brother. His needs are my needs, his interests are my interests, and I want to have fellowship with him, no matter who he is or what the circumstances are under which he lives. *Love* is the most important response.
2. The second response is that of regarding him as *negligible*. That is, a person can be so self-centered that in his world there is no room for anybody else, and he has drawn the curtain, he has closed the door and locked the window. Life is built solely around himself.
3. We can regard the other man as a *nuisance*. Any giving or

sharing that we do or are called on to make for those less fortunate gives us a pain in the neck.

4. We can regard him with *contempt,* which is a step further in the wrong direction. The other man is a necessary, though lesser, breed. He is unimportant, that is, compared with our dignity and our prestige.

5. We can regard him as an outright *enemy.*

So, you see, you travel the scale from love to considering a person your enemy.

The musical, *Bandwagon,* serves as a confession of modern man's predicament and the reason for his frustration. Here is a telling statement that is made in it which illustrates my point. One says, "Here we are, the only animals given speech, and here we are, snarling at each other!"

In medieval poetry and drama the seven deadly sins were usually represented by animals. Medieval man thought of himself as a son of God with an eternal destiny, but striving with the animal in him. Modern man leaves out the idea of himself as a son of God and is content to be the animal.

Look at the procession of the animals representing the sins in medieval literature: *pride* is variously represented as a lion, peacock, eagle, horse, or bull; *envy* as a dog, snake, wolf, dragon, board, or toad; *anger* as a wolf, toad, pig, rat, rooster, dragon, or snake; *avarice* as a wolf, fox, hawk, elephant, ass, spider, or snake; and down the scales these medievals went.

"Here we are, the only animals given the power of speech, and here we are, snarling at one another." John puts his finger on one of the greatest needs of Christian people in the world today.

I. MURDER—HOMICIDE

First John 3:15 very clearly and plainly states: "Whosoever hateth his brother is a *murderer.* And you know that no murderer has eternal life abiding in him." God says that *whosoever hateth* is a murderer. Now, who does not know something of the growth of personal hostility and how it snowballs? A slight wrong is done, perhaps entirely unintentional, but it is done, and then it begins to color our judgment and every response that we make. We are prone to shun, to ignore, to refuse to speak, to gossip about, and to imagine that people hate us, and we, in turn, hate them more and we impute evil motives to the things they do. Who does not know? Such ought to be left to the man in the street (bad enough for him), the man who does not even profess faith in Jesus Christ; but when it comes into the circle of God's people it's a crying shame and tragic sin!

I know some church people who won't even speak to other church people. I know some professing Christians who seem to be pained just to speak to the pastor, to the minister. Who does not know that these things have a way of developing and growing within us, and, my friend, this is not mere picturesque hyperbole.

Listen to our Lord. In the Sermon on the Mount Jesus says:

> Ye have heard that it was said by them of old time, Thou shall not kill; and whosoever shall kill shall be in danger of the judgment: But I say unto you, That whosoever is *angry* with his brother without a cause shall be in danger of the judgment.
>
> . . . .
>
> Therefore if thou bring thy gift to the altar, and there remember that thy brother hath aught against thee; leave there thy gift. . . .

"Don't try to worship me," God says. "If you've got anything in your heart that separates you from any man, don't you try to worship me until you have first gone and tried to become reconciled to that person."

Or, again, you have heard it said, "Thou shalt love thy neighbour and hate thine enemy. But I say unto you, Love your enemies, bless them that curse you, do good to them that hate you, pray for them which despitefully use you, and persecute you."

No, this is not picturesque hyperbole. We are talking about the gospel of Jesus Christ. Remember, there is *no feeling within* which can be dissipated until it finds expression in some way. And the most awful effects of hatred that I know are to be seen in the murder of the world's blessed Redeemer. That was no accidental end that came to Jesus Christ; it was the inevitable end in a world like ours, and with people who were human beings. It was inevitable.

We have a way of nursing grudges, of harboring feelings against others. And it's rather sobering to realize that there never has been a single hateful thought which we have entertained that has not gone back to swell the reservoir within; which is bound, sooner or later, to reach floodstage and then to break the bounds that hold it. And this hate never finds satisfaction until it nails Jesus Christ in derision to the cross. *"Whosoever hateth is a murderer."*

II. SUICIDE: DARKNESS

The second word is "suicide." Hate has a way of affecting our brother against whom it is directed, but especially it affects us. It might eventually end in murdering another person, but think of what it does to us, to people who hate. Tragic headlines fill the papers day after day with the end, the fruitage, of hate, where husband and wife hate each other so intensely, or a parent and child, or neighbor and neighbor—whatever the case might be— hate each other so intensely that it breaks the bounds and then murder and suicide result.

Think with me, for instance, of the physical effects of harboring hatred and enmity and all these related things. I want to quote here; I'm not the authority, I have copied from the pens of others these statements so I cannot verify them.

Here is a doctor, W. P. Newsholme, in his book, *Health, Disease and Integration,* who said: "Hate is poison, not only moral and spiritual poison, but mental and physical poison as well. A mother was suckling with resentment and hate toward another. The child dropped dead on her breast—poisoned by the hate which had got into the mother's milk."

Dr. E. Stanley Jones, in his book, *Is the Kingdom of God Realism?* says that a prominent surgeon in a large university in America said to him: "I have discovered the kingdom of God at the point of my scalpel. It is written in the tissues. The right thing is always the healthy thing."

The *British Medical Journal* gives this dictum: "There is not a tissue in the human body wholly removed from the influence of the spirit."

A famous surgeon told Dr. Stanley Jones that 90 percent of the people who came to him for operations could have been cured without surgery if they had had the right moral and spiritual attitudes toward life. The diseases would have been headed off— they were largely functional before they became organic.

Two years ago, Mrs. Parker and I had the privilege of being in Uganda, Africa, where we saw the natives in the area of Moroto. In this particular region the natives have weird customs, such as dressing in cowhide. This is the only clothing that the women wore; just dirty, stinking, heavy old cowhide. But then they had all sorts of trinkets made of metal hanging from their ears, nose, lips—burdens that disfigured and hurt them. And yet we, at the same time, refuse to forgive and carry these burdens on our hearts and in our souls, failing to realize that *they hurt us.*

Haman, in the book of Esther, is a perfect illustration of this in the Bible. Haman was the Prime Minister of Persia, under the wicked king Ahaziah. Everybody feared Haman. Everywhere he went people got down on the ground and groveled before him, *except one*—old Mordecai, stiff-necked, proud leader of the Jews. Mordecai refused to do this and it was more than Haman could take, so he built a gallows five cubits high, the Bible tells us, and his intention was to hang Mordecai on it and then destroy the entire Jewish race, held captive in the land. Well, you remember the story, and the end of it was that Haman, himself, was hanged on his gallows, and the wind blew his body so all could see it.

Two neighbors had a falling out, and one of them said, "I'll get even with him!" So he built a fence twenty feet high between them. Not only did it shut out his neighbor's face, but it also shut out the sun from his own life. So you see, there are physical effects and also spiritual effects.

Booker T. Washington made a statement that is quoted so much, but how pertinent it becomes here: "I will not permit any man to so narrow and degrade my soul as to make me hate him."

Do you remember Amos and Andy? Amos was the little fellow with some crazy ideas, and yet, how human he was. Andy knew a big fellow who, every time he would come near him, would slap him in the chest with the back of his hand. Andy just took all of it he could until one day he said to Amos: "I'm going to fix him! I'm ready for him the next time he hits me. I'll put a stick of dynamite in my vest pocket and the next time he slaps me he's going to get his hand blowed off!"

Ah, yes, in so much of our relationship with each other we are like this. You know, Jesus said something very significant here. He said: "Agree with thine adversary quickly, whilst thou art with him in the way." Why? Because he knew that when resentment festers, it becomes poison. There is an inward deterioration and its worst effects simply put us in total darkness. That is why.

III. FORGIVENESS

Oh, but there is another word. The first one is *murder,* the second one is *suicide,* or what it does to us, but the beautiful word is the word, *forgiveness.* It has a musical ring about it, doesn't it? And have you ever stopped to think about the direct relationship that word has to Divine forgiveness where you and I are concerned? I'm talking about our relationship to each other; how directly connected our attitudes toward each other are with our relationship to God. No duty is so frequently enjoined in the Word of God upon the children of God as the necessity of forgiveness!

For instance, Paul said: "If thine enemy hunger, feed him; if he thirst, give him drink; for in so doing thou shalt heap coals of fire on his head. Be not overcome of evil, but overcome evil with good" (Rom. 12:20–21). Paul also said: "Be ye kind to one another, tenderhearted, forgiving one another, even as God for Christ's sake hath forgiven you" (Eph. 4:32). He also said: "Forbearing one another, and forgiving one another; if any man have a quarrel against any: even as Christ forgave you, so also do ye" (Col. 3:13).

Our Lord said: "If thy brother trespass against thee, rebuke him; and if he repent, forgive him. And if he trespass against thee *seven times in a day,* and seven times in a day turn again to thee saying, I repent; thou shalt forgive him."

And then, that matchless prayer that our Lord gave to his disciples. You remember that right in the middle of it is the petition, "forgive us our debts, as we forgive our debtors." Do you know what you pray when you pray that prayer? You deliberately ask God in an indirect way not to forgive you, if you harbor anything against a fellowman.

Have you ever read that story about Robert Louis Stevenson and that petition? He had the custom in his family of having family worship *every day.* And, no matter what passage of Scripture they had studied, nor what the prayers were, they always concluded their meditation and prayer with the Lord's Prayer. One night when they came to that petition, Robert Louis Stevenson jumped up and stormed out of the room. His wife got up and followed him because she thought he was ill. When she reached him she said, "What is the matter? Are you ill?" And his response was, "No, I'm not really ill. I'm just not fit to pray that prayer."

When General Oglethorpe was Governor of Georgia, during the

days of John Wesley, he talked with Wesley one day and said: "I *never* forgive." Whereupon John Wesley said to him, "Well, in that case, I hope you never sin!"

My friend, it's just that simple. In order for God to forgive us, we must have the right kind of attitude toward others. Now, that's the necessity; but I want to look for just a moment at the peace, the happiness, the joy, and the real peace of mind that comes to a person who has a forgiving spirit. Actually, I've often felt that a forgiving spirit can do more for some people than a prolonged stay in a hospital. It has a way of working miracles in a person's life, if he will let God's spirit come in and control his attitudes and his words, instead of being sharp and critical and divisive and disgruntled and mean. What a difference! It was old Mark Twain who said one day: "Forgiveness is the fragrance the violet sheds on the heel that crushes it." This is beautiful!

There is no such thing as forgiving without *forgetting.* If you say that you can't forget, that is a pretty good indication that you haven't forgiven in the first place, because that's not the way God does things and that's not the way God commands that you and I do them. The Bible tells us: "Be ye kind one to another, tender-hearted, forgiving one another even as God for Christ's sake hath forgiven you." How does God forgive? Well, the Bible also tells us that he not only forgives, but he forgets. "I will forgive their iniquity, and I will remember their sin *no more.*" That's the way God does it, and that's the way he commands that you and I do it.

William J. Gaynor was mayor of the City of New York many years ago. He had many bitter enemies, people who did everything they could to embarrass him, to fight him, and make very kind of accusation against him. One time he had started on a vacation and somebody even shot him down on the deck of the ship. But do you know what his philosophy was? Here it is: "I forgive *everyone, everything, every day.*" You can get that kind of spirit only through the presence of God's spirit in your heart and life. Think of what it cost him to be able to forgive you and me. It cost him everything. And he can love us and save us simply because he was willing to give everything in order to be able to forgive us.

It doesn't cost you and me anything to try to live in the Spirit of Christ and to be forgiving, and loving, and to push hatred and anger and resentment out of our hearts and let the Holy Spirit come in. He can't live there if these things are in us, because our lives are the temple where he longs to dwell.

He may be speaking to you right now, and I know of only one solution to the misery that grips so many today, and that is to get right with the Lord, to let Christ come into your heart and life, let him make a new person out of you, and let his Spirit come daily with freshness and love and power into your life. Make that decision right now!

10.

Walking in the Light

(1 John 1)

Certainly 1 John 1 is one of the greatest chapters in the Bible with which to begin anew. Listen to John: "God is light, and in him is no darkness at all. . . . If we walk in the light, as he is in the light, we have fellowship one with another, and the blood of Jesus Christ his Son cleanseth us from all sin."

I. A MAGNIFICENT METAPHOR: GOD IS LIGHT!

John's magnificent metaphor, "God is light," reminds us so much of what he said in his Gospel, in the first chapter:

"In the beginning was the Word, and the Word was with God, and the Word was God. The same was in the beginning with God. All things were made by him; and without him was not anything made that was made. In him was life; and the life was the light of men. And the light shineth in darkness; and the darkness comprehended it not. There was a man sent from God, whose name was John. The same came for a witness, to bear witness of the Light, that all men through him might believe. He was not that Light [that is, John was not], but was sent to bear witness of that Light. That was the true Light, which lighteth every man that cometh into the world" (vv. 1–9).

"God is Light, and in him is no darkness at all" (1 John 1:5).

The coming of the Messiah is pictured for us repeatedly in the Bible as the Light to illumine the world's darkness. For instance, Isaiah 9:2: "The people that walked in darkness have seen a great light: they that dwell in the land of the shadow of death, upon them hath the light shined."

"Then spake Jesus again unto them, saying, I am the light of the world: he that followeth me shall not walk in darkness, but shall have the light of life" (John 8:12).

"Yet a little while is the light with you. Walk while ye have the light, lest darkness come upon you: for he that walketh in darkness knoweth not whither he goeth" (John 12:35).

"For God, who commanded the light to shine out of darkness, hath shined in our hearts, to give the light of the knowledge of the glory of God in the face of Jesus Christ" (2 Cor. 4:6).

"Wherefore he saith, Awake thou that sleepest, and arise from the dead, and Christ shall give thee light" (Eph. 5:14).

Now, the gospel records indicate to us, and emphasize the fact, that it was night when Jesus was born. For instance, they tell us about the shepherds keeping watch over their flocks by night. They tell us about the Wise Men following the star to the cradle where the infant Savior was to be found. They tell us about Herod's gloomy midnight councils, when the plotting and the planning were done for the slaughter of the infants in Bethlehem. And against this encompassing darkness, Christ's coming shone out. What the records say in symbol, Phillips Brooks later sang in song:

> Yet in thy dark streets shineth
> The everlasting light;
> The hopes and fears of all the years
> Are met in Thee tonight.

I love the song which we often sing in our church:

> The whole world was lost in the darkness of sin,

The Light of the world is Jesus;
Like sunshine at noonday His glory shone in,
The Light of the world is Jesus.

No darkness have we who in Jesus abide,
We walk in the light when we follow our guide.

Ye dwellers in darkness with sin-blinded eyes,
Go, wash, at His bidding, and light will arise.

No need of the sunlight in heaven we're told,
The Lamb is the Light in the city of gold.

Come to the Light, 'tis shining for thee;
Sweetly the Light has dawned upon me,
Once I was blind, but now I can see:
The Light of the world is Jesus.

God is Light. Jesus said, "I am the light of the world: he that followeth me shall not walk in darkness, but shall have the light of life."

Now, what is the meaning of this metaphor? Well, light is the natural, universal symbol of deity. Anywhere in religious writings you come upon the term "light" you know that there is some inference, some indication of deity involved. But, as John uses it here, there is far more involved, because the word has an ethical content, and it emphasizes the moral character of God, for God is wholly good, and completely untouched by evil. Jesus said, "Be ye therefore perfect, even as your Father which is in heaven is perfect."

The symbols employed in this great chapter are *light* and *darkness;* divine light for men's darkness. And they are common symbols, too, for they indicate something to us about man's ignorance over against God's infinite knowledge; man's limited powers and abilities as over against God's unlimited understanding and powers; omniscience as over against human limitations.

> Our little systems have their day;
>> They have their day and cease to be:
>> They are but broken lights of Thee,
> And Thou, O Lord, art more than they.

The symbol involved is that of the contrast between righteousness and sin. In all great religions the idea of the contrast between light and darkness pictures for mankind the conflict between good and evil, between right and wrong, between sin and righteousness. Now, you remember Paul's statement in Ephesians 6: "For we wrestle not against flesh and blood, but against principalities, against powers, against the rulers of darkness of this world, against spiritual wickedness in high places." These are the symbols of light and darkness.

But, my friend, when you say that Jesus Christ is the Light of the world, you are talking about what Jesus has done for the world, and for mankind, and these writers try to tell us over and over again about how Jesus brought them out of darkness into his marvelous light. It was a monk in the Middle Ages who made this remark about his own conversion: "It was as if, in the middle of a dark night, day suddenly broke."

> Two thousand years ago at Bethlehem,
>> God lit a candle: to its radiant light
>> Came men from near and far.
> It still lights up the darkness of the world,
>> Still to the heights of men who come to seek,
> It is the Guiding Star.

What has he done for our world as the Light of the world? Well, he has banished darkness from the very face of God.

It is interesting to go back to chapter 8 of John's Gospel, verse 12, where Jesus said, "I am the Light of the world." Remember the circumstances that were involved. It was the Feast of Tabernacles. It was that time of year when the Jewish nation observed the forty years' wandering in the wilderness through a sacred feast day, symbolizing God's presence and leadership in the form of a pillar of smoke by day and a pillar of fire by night. It was on that occasion that Jesus stood to say, "I am the light of the world." By that he simply means that he reveals God. He shows us God. Paul said, "We have seen the glory of God in the face of Jesus Christ." He said to his own disciples, "He that hath seen me hath seen the Father."

And so, he lights up God for man's benefit. He reveals God to mankind and we come to know what God is like when we see him in the face of Jesus Christ. "God hath shined in our hearts, giving us the light of the knowledge of his glory in the face of Jesus Christ." He banished the darkness from the face of God to show us what God is like.

He also has banished the darkness from the face of the world in which you and I live. Now, this does not mean that everything that is foul, lewd, base, and wrong has been banished from the earth. That isn't what it means at all. What it means is that people who have seen his light, people who know God through his radiant face, know that he has banished falsehood and the glamor of the things that are wrong in our world, and revealed them for what they actually are. There is still falsehood, but God's people understand the wrong involved in falsehood because of the life that we have through Jesus Christ. The same can be said about selfishness, greed, injustice, war, or any of the thousand things that are wrong with our world. No, he has not banished these things, but he has banished the darkness and shown them for what they are.

May I use a current illustration? As of midnight, January 2, 1971, no more cigarette advertisements can be shown on television or broadcast on radio. That does not mean that cigarettes have been banned; that doesn't mean that they have been done away with; but by law now, the truth has to be told openly, publicly; and all of the glamor that has been pictured to us has been stripped away and people who have eyes to see can see cigarettes for what they are. That is exactly the way God has banished darkness from our world. He has shown us wrong in its true light. He has banished darkness from the very face of eternity. Think about the world into which Jesus came, about the hopelessness of life, about the despair when people laid their loved ones away and turned aside from open graves, without hope, without any prospect beyond the grave. "Farewell" was one of the chief words placed on their tombstones. Oh, but when Jesus Christ came and lived and died, and was resurrected from the grave, all of this was changed because he said: "I go to prepare a place for you. And if I go and prepare a place for you, I will come again, and receive you unto myself; that where I am, there ye may be also." The teachings of God's Word from that time on shine with radiant splendor about the future of God's children, of believers in Christ.

Now look at the metaphor again and what it means to us: "God is *light,* and in him is no darkness at all."

II. THE DIVINE IMPERATIVE: WALK IN THE LIGHT!

John now gives us an imperative in the light of that great truth. John says that we ought to walk "in the light." Now, light is absolutely luminous and transparent. Nothing can be hidden, and nothing needs to be hidden where light is involved, so "walk in the light" means then to live a life in which nothing is hidden.

Listen to our Lord:

And this is the condemnation, that light is come into the world, and men loved darkness rather than light, because their deeds were evil.

For every one that doeth evil hateth the light, neither cometh to the light, lest his deeds should be reproved.

But he that doeth truth cometh to the light, that his leeds may be made manifest, that they are wrought in

God.

And when a person comes to the light, the first thing that happens in his life is that prompt and complete confession must be made, because sin cannot endure in the presence of the light. The first impulse in the human heart, however, is to hide it. The first impulse is to try to forget it, to suppress it, and this is one reason why there are so many distraught, unhappy, divided personalities in society today. It is because of the mountain of sin that we suppress in our own souls and carry about with us every hour of the day. A boy with dirty hands will avoid his mother, as the crook will avoid the lights of the city at night, because sin has a way of clinging to the shadows and the darkness. David sang long ago, "When I kept silence my bones waxed old within me."

But Oh, the moment we come into the light, what happens to us? Let me give you one illustration. Zacchaeus was up a sycamore tree and Jesus came and stopped under the tree. Zacchaeus came down at the command of Jesus and, standing there with everything stripped away, he was face to face with the Son of God. Listen to him: "Oh, Lord, if I have wronged any man," and he knew full well he had wronged many a person, "If I have wronged any man, I will repay him fourfold."

Listen, my friend, prompt and complete confession of sin takes place when a person walks into the presence of divine light. It means that we are going to take Jesus Christ as our example. John says; "Walk in the light as he is in the light." "Come ye after me," Jesus said, "And I will make you to become fishers of men."

Now, from the basic conviction about God, *God is Light,* John draws a conclusion about believers. Don't miss this: *The profession of one's relationship to God must be attested by the character which one lives.* That is the whole thing.

Dr. Malcolm Tolbert says: "The verb 'walk' is a Hebraism. It comprehends the total experience of an individual—his thinking, speaking, living, acting and his interacting as a human being." [1]

In other words, "walk" stresses the vital relationship between belief and behavior!

Out on the mission field we endeavored as earnestly and simply as we knew how to present the gospel so that the native, without any education or training, could understand what we were talking about. I found that one of the favorite expressions in evangelism on the mission field is to talk to them in terms of "walking the Jesus Road." That's not a bad expression, is it? When a person comes into the knowledge of Jesus Christ, into the light of God as shed in the face of Jesus; when a person professes faith in Jesus Christ, Christ ought to become his example, and he ought to walk, then, on "the Jesus Road."

What does this imply? It implies taking morality seriously. If you are going to walk in the light of Jesus Christ, this implies taking morality seriously, because Jesus Christ is the fullest expression in history of what it means to live a responsible, moral life, under God. He is the most perfect illustration that can be found. You talk about the new morality, or situation ethics, but what I'm appealing to you to do is not so much to take a creed or a code and live by it—as valuable as that might be—but to take a *person,* and live by his will and his example. Don't ask yourself whether a course of action is right for you under certain circumstances, but ask yourself the question: "What would Jesus do under these circumstances?" To follow Jesus Christ, to walk in the light, means to take morality seriously, to recognize our utter and complete dependence upon him for everything that we need and everything that comes into our hands.

In the fifteenth chapter of John, Jesus puts it this way; in this marvelous chapter on the vine and the branches, he said:

Abide in me, and I in you, As the branch cannot bear
fruit of itself, except it abide in the vine; no more can ye,
except ye abide in me.

I am the vine, ye are the branches: He that abideth in

me, and I in him, the same bringeth forth much fruit: for
without me ye can do nothing.

If a man abide not in me, he is cast forth as a branch,
and is withered; and men gather them, and cast them into
the fire, and they are burned.

If ye abide in me, and my words abide in you, ye shall
ask what ye will, and it shall be done unto you.

Recognize our utter and complete dependence upon Jesus Christ
for everything that you need, and he will supply it. You remember
that marvelous statement Isaiah made in chapter 40 of his
prophecy: "They that wait upon the Lord shall renew their
strength; they shall mount up with wings as eagles; they shall run,
and not be weary; they shall walk, and not faint." If you study that
passage carefully, you will find that the most difficult thing mentioned is that of walking—hour after hour, day after day, in the
light of the countenance of Jesus Christ, and literally living the
Word of God, and literally living the will of God. "Abide in me,"
is what Jesus commands that we do.

It also demands that we relate ourselves to the ongoing of con-
tinuing ministry of Jesus Christ in our world, for he said, "As the
Father hath sent me, even so send I you." "Follow me, and I will
make you to become fishers of men." "Ye are my witnesses."

III. PERENNIAL NEEDS OF MAN FULFILLED
BY "WALKING IN THE LIGHT"

Look at the metaphor again: "God is light, and in him is no
darkness at all." Now, our imperative is that we walk in the light.
At this point John refers to some perennial needs of man's heart,
things that happen when people walk in the light, and these are
conditioned upon our walking in the light.

In the first place is *fellowship.* "If we walk in the light as he is
in the light, we have fellowship." There are two kinds of fellowship

mentioned in this chapter; one of them is fellowship with each other, and the other is fellowship with God. Both of them are contingent upon our walking in the light. Fellowship is one of the rich and spacious words in the Bible, literally filled with suggestiveness. The word means: "distribution, communication, communion, partakers, partners, companions." In other words, to have all things in common. I think we can boil our deep aspirations down to one deep-felt yearning and longing for the human heart: a complete and permanent human fellowship in our world. This is the ideal, and it exists in every department in life—in the family, in civic life, in commercial life, in national life, and on the international plane. Indeed, history is nothing on earth except the story of a world blindly struggling towards this ideal, beginning with the family, moving on to the tribe and the clan, the nation, and eventually the United Nations—a real international fellowship, a brotherhood of all men. The deep longing of our hearts is that there might be peace and understanding in our world, and real fellowship between people and between nations.

Who can measure the value of fellowship, even on the plane of person to person. Who really can measure the value? I like what I came across the other day in a book entitled, *Life for a Life,* written by Mrs. Dinah Maria Mulock Craik. In it she is talking about fellowship and says this:

> "Oh, the comfort, the inexpressible comfort of feeling safe with a person. Having neither to waste thoughts nor measure words, but pour them all right out just as they are, chaff and grain together, knowing that a faithful hand will take and sift them, keeping what is worth keeping, and with the breath of kindness, blow the rest away."

How many people are there in whose company you can pour out everything in your heart, say everything you want to say, withhold absolutely nothing, say anything? I dare say there are very few with whom you enjoy that kind of fellowship. And yet, all of us hunger for it. But, my friend, there is a deeper fellowship and a more meaningful one than that of person-to-person, and this is on the divine level. The fellowship which men seek is an illusive thing, really, simply because it does not go deep enough. It is based, usually, upon the relative, the incidental thing, and it seems to be very hard for man to learn that vital and meaningful fellowship must have an essential, spiritual, eternal basis. That is exactly what the Christian gospel is all about. That's what we proclaim to the world; that a fellowship based in God is the meaningful kind of fellowship. When we "walk in the light, as he is in the light, then we have fellowship with him, and we can have fellowship with one another," because our fellowship is based upon a solid, spiritual foundation.

Wouldn't it be good if every reader of this book were to decide to do all in his power to deepen his spiritual life through a closer walk with the Lord, so that it might be written about each one what was written about Enoch: "Enoch walked with God, and was not, for God took him." Or, what was written about Moses: "Moses, whom the Lord knew face to face. . . ." Jesus longs for that kind of fellowship, that kind of communion, that kind of partnership. Listen:

> "Behold, I stand at the door and knock: if any man hear my voice, and open the door, I will come in to him, and will sup with him, and he with me."
> "If we walk in the light as he is in the light, we have *fellowship*. . . ."

But now there is something else involved, in referring to the basic needs of every life. One need is for fellowship, the other is for *cleansing*. We have fellowship with God, and also cleansing from our sins. The verb that is used is in the present tense, indicating a continuous action all through the year, and indeed all through life. That has reference to nothing on earth except the sanctification of the believer in and through Jesus Christ. As dreadful as the power of sin is in our world, there is a power that is greater—far greater—and this is the blood of Jesus Christ. "For where sin abounded, grace did much more abound."

My friend, God is concerned about our purification, just as he is concerned about our communion or our fellowship with him. God is Light. Walk in the Light so that you can have fellowship and continuous cleansing.

Now, if we believe in him Who is the Light of the world, if we walk in the Light as he is in the Light, if we let our light so shine before men that others can see our good works and glorify our Father who is in heaven, then one of God's days we will be brought to that City of Light, where there is no darkness, where there is no unhappiness, no heartache, no pain, no suffering, no death.

The writer, in his vision on Patmos, tells us that the Lamb is the Light thereof; the same one who said, "I am the Light of the world." And so, through establishing a vital contact with him, and then walking with him through this world, one day you will go home to live in the Light which he gives.

---

[1] Malcolm Tolbert, *Walking in the Light* (Nashville: Broadman Press, 1970).

252
Par

CLASS   ACC.

Parker, Henry) Allen

(LAST NAME OF AUTHOR)

Living At Peace In A Turbulent
                                    World

(BOOK TITLE)

PARK CITY BAPTIST CHURCH
PARK CITY, KENTUCKY

STAMP LIBRARY OWNERSHIP

CODE 4386-03   BROADMAN SUPPLIES
CLS-3   MADE IN U. S. A.